THE
ENCHANTED
COTTAGE

The Enchanted Cottage

DEBBIE A RADFORD

ISBN: 979-8-9900451-1-8

Editor: Dylan Radford

Cover Artist
Felipe Gimenez Zapiola | felipegimzap.com | @felipegimzap

Interior Chapter Artist (pages 1, 44, 82, 116, 154, 196, 254)
Annalyse Lucero | @aluceromft

Floor Plan Artist
Patrick Arguelles

To the ones who never stop wishing,
no matter how many stars it takes.

CONTENTS

CONTENT ADVISORY

This book explores themes that may be
sensitive for some readers including:

grief & loss,
pregnancy loss &
miscarriage,
infertility,
depression,
anxiety,
friendship loss
sexual trauma,
sexually explicit content,
& possibly more.

Please be advised and practice
self-care while reading.

At the Forest's Edge

The sun dips low,
casting citrine blushes
through towering trees.

My husband, my child, and I
tread the winding path,
eager for rest.

Before us stands
The Enchanted Cottage,
nestled in nature's embrace—
ivy, jasmine, and wildflowers
welcoming us like old friends.

The door creaks open—
an oak-kissed threshold—
to a place where love
might find its shelter again
in a tender embrace.

Inside, magic breathes.
The hearth is warm;
the garden alive.

Like a sanctuary,
the stones are ready to unravel
the tangled threads of grief.

Through windows aglow,
the evening light filters in—
it dances upon the walls.
Each flicker a promise
of the wonder yet to come.

The air hums with nostalgia and stories—
lessons and possibilities.

Laughter and tears
melted into the very wood.

The tree's branches sing songs
of living and joy,
and beneath our feet,
the veranda creaks in rhythmic patterns—
as if the cottage's screeches and scrapings
were a spoken beckon to enter.

Hand in hand,
we step within,
hoping
that perhaps,

               magic is real.

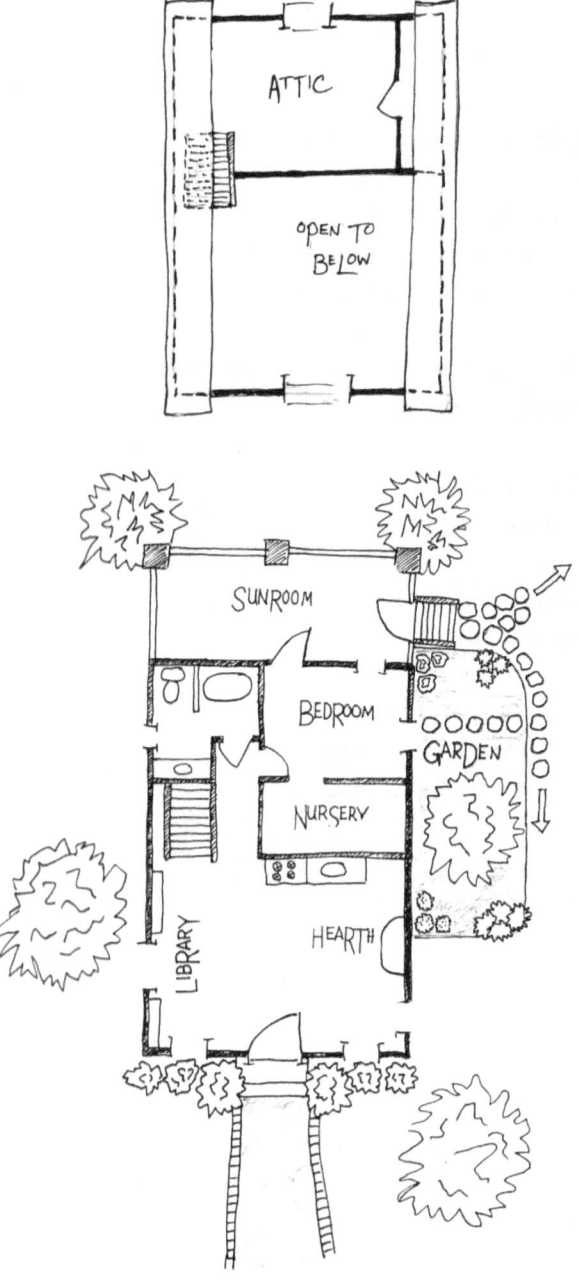

ATTIC

OPEN TO
BELOW

SUNROOM

BEDROOM

NURSERY

GARDEN

LIBRARY

HEARTH

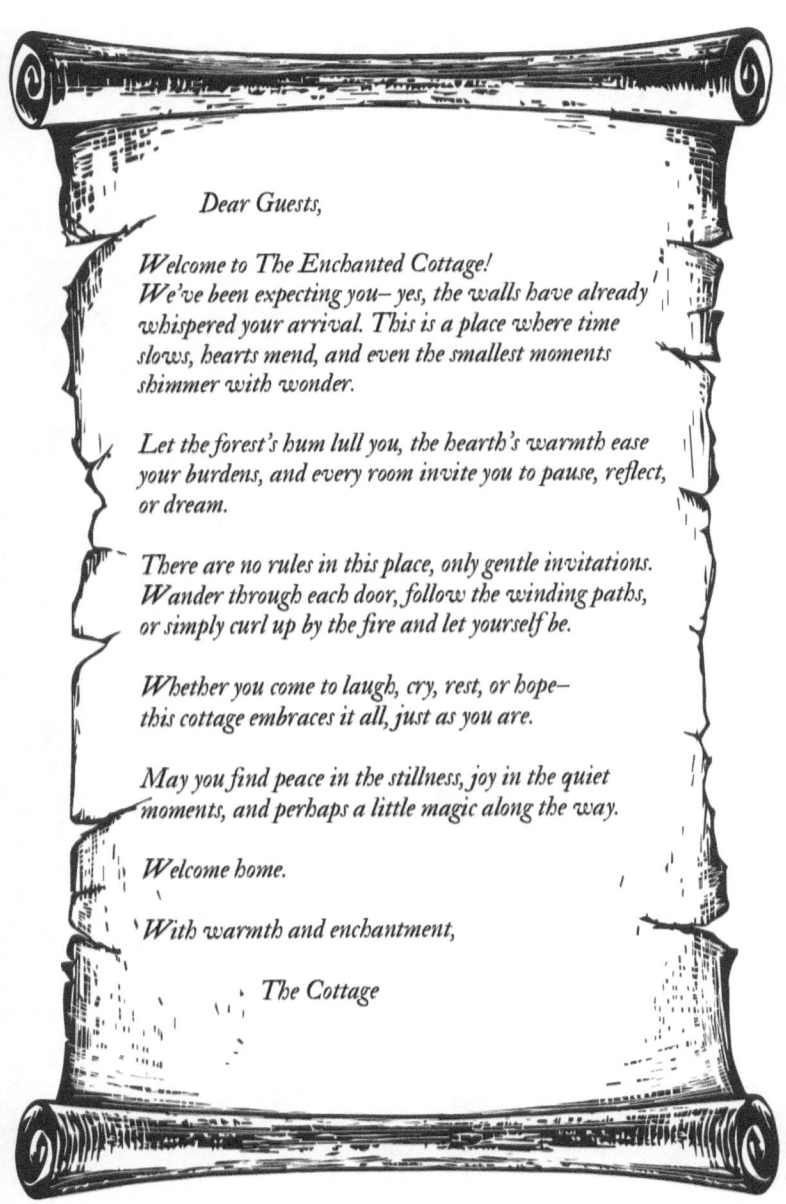

Dear Guests,

Welcome to The Enchanted Cottage!
We've been expecting you— yes, the walls have already
whispered your arrival. This is a place where time
slows, hearts mend, and even the smallest moments
shimmer with wonder.

Let the forest's hum lull you, the hearth's warmth ease
your burdens, and every room invite you to pause, reflect,
or dream.

There are no rules in this place, only gentle invitations.
Wander through each door, follow the winding paths,
or simply curl up by the fire and let yourself be.

Whether you come to laugh, cry, rest, or hope—
this cottage embraces it all, just as you are.

May you find peace in the stillness, joy in the quiet
moments, and perhaps a little magic along the way.

Welcome home.

With warmth and enchantment,

   The Cottage

CHAPTER ONE

The Hearth

No Turning Back

This change,
a mysterious harbinger,
arrives not with a gentle gesture,
but a trembling roar,
and the unknown tightens its grip
on my yearning to hold the reins.

I look back to the closing door—
familiarity clings like comfort—
old routines call back.

It wasn't *that* bad, was it- the humdrum?

Yet my heart races
a curious craving,
and the change beckons— it rumbles.

Sometimes we don't need
a comforting cradle,
but a shoulder shake.

Wake up! Change growls.

And my soul answers
in a returning resonance,
because it knows,

it was *that* bad,
and there is no turning back.

OLD LETTERS

It was an echo of old letters,
worn and weathered,
inscribed with instructions
in forgotten languages.
Their meanings slipping
through the cracks of time–
like sand through open fingers.
The drawer opens up,
fresh parchment flying out–
a summon
to write a new beginning.

For when the past slumbers,
a new beginning may be awakened.

The Hearth

What wounds linger
at the table within the hearth–
where the flicker of a stovetop
holds our deepest tears?

It must hear the silence
of unspoken heartaches
and worries that crackle
in the quiet of the dark.

Does it feel the warmth
of our coupled embrace
as we huddle close
on sleepless nights?

Does it dance with the laughter
of tiny, skipping feet,
and find solace in
the soft hum of a lullaby?

Oh, the stories it could share
if only it could speak.
The hearth knows
all the secrets
we keep.

OVERSTIMULATED

I'm short of breath.
It's an overwhelming,
arduous,
backbreaking
anxiety–
mounting like ivy,
towering into messy discomfort.

I long for peace–
sunlight dancing
through open windows.

I long for order
amidst the chaos.

For a sanctuary
where the only clutter
is the gentle tumble
of petals on the floor,
and the only tension
is the weight
of a butterfly
on my hand.

WHEN LEAST EXPECTED

A stray beam of sunlight
slipped through the cracked door
like a melody
finding its way into silence–
                          surprising and sweet.

The best gifts
can sometimes be the ones
you didn't know you needed.

Popcorn and a Movie

Cuddled up on a chenille couch,
with a fleece blanket
draped over our tangled legs,
I could feel the piercing of your eye
silently telling me to put my phone down.

I think I've seen this movie
a thousand times,
but I've never actually watched it.

How often do we get caught up in the
missing out
that we actually
miss out
on the moment we are in?

Why do we look through another window
that stares out into nothing?

How many movies have I missed?

I clutch the blanket a little tighter,
nuzzle my toes towards yours
to let you know I'm *really* here this time,
and we share a bowl of popcorn.

Right Now

There is only right now,
and I don't want to miss it.

I refuse to blunder the summer's sunset
casting marvels in your eyes,
or the way you just looked at me–
a smile blooming on your lips.

I refuse to miss
our toes dancing
to the song of the wind,
and the seamless feel
of your hand in mine.

I won't dwell in yesterday's grief,
or be shadowed
by tomorrow's doubt.
I want to be here,
with you,
right now.

Birthday Candles

I wish...
for the kind of happiness
that surfaces on quiet Sunday mornings.
In the aroma of freshly brewed coffee,
and in the comfort of knowing
I've lived another day
true to myself.

CHAOS OF FULLNESS

We are juggling
sunshine and moonlight
with open arms,
and heavy eyelids.

I walk beneath the open sky,
and harvest laughter for the days
that will be filled with fatigue.

Those buds of giggles fuel me
when my mind wants to drift.

It's in the chaos of fullness
that her smile refreshes my heart–
like misty coolness.

Even in this tired light
I clutch the glow.
I would never trade
this loud living
for a quiet longing.

Lucky Star

The evening stirs
as the scent of dinner lingers,
and she asks for a familiar melody.
Among the carousel of tunes,
Lucky Star waits.

A beat pulses–
its glow dripping into the room,
like iridescent wishes.

The song breathes–
fills the air with silver sparkles,
and soon we're all dancing
under a silly sky.

We twirl in dizzy joy
where our hands are constellations–
holding the universe between our fingers.

Our feet flutter,
spinning in giggles and wishes
as the ceiling melts
into a sea of midnight.

A flicker above–
our makeshift stars sway.

The twinkling light bulb
above our heads,
the one we'll fix someday,
but never soon enough.

For now, it's our disco ball in the clouds.

Starlight, star bright,
make everything alright.

And I think,
beneath the weightless sky of joy,
this is the dream people speak of
when they make wishes
upon a *lucky star.*

WILDSONG

In the silence between the pines,
our hearts beat like distant drums,
tuned to the wildsong of wind and leaf.
Where no one asks us to be anything
but the soft rustle of ourselves.

We lay our burdens beneath the boughs.
The world's demands fading,
as the sky sings us whole.

Here, the only truth is
the laughter of our child,
the flutter of her joy–
boundless.

We let the world spin on its tired axis.
We are rooted here, in the soil of now.
Our feet trace the earth like a melody–
hands held tight
with the chorus of all that matters.

The wildsong hums of freedom–
of love untamed
by the noise of expectation.
We are the music,
alive in the moment, enough, *together*,
and singing with the trees.

SIMPLE HAPPINESS

It's a simple happiness–
our hearts unburdened,
light,
and free,
basking in a joyful moment
we get to keep.

Great Magic

There is no greater magic
in this world
then in knowing,
no matter where
our earthly existence takes us,
we will always
hold one another's light
within our hearts.

Quiet Warmth

Beneath the low mumble of burning logs,
warmth unfurls like quiet breathing.
It binds the cracks in the walls,
and the fractures in our hearts.

The scent of pine,
carried on an inhale of firelight,
lingers in the corners
where shadows once loomed,
now softened by a golden hue.

Here, in the dance of glow and wood,
the quiet sway of a flame
knows the art of mending,
as it stitches us back together
in the spaces where words fall short.

Secrets by the Fire

Does she know our fireside secrets?
See the glow casting shadows
under our eyes,
or the weight of our hearts wishing
love's warmth would slowly
melt the grief away.

I hope she knows love endures.

Does she see the ashes
holding the remnants of the longing
we've burned and released, once more?

*I hope she can see
the strength in vulnerability.*

Does she hear the wind chimes on the porch,
echoing desires we sing to the night sky,
or how we look out the window
at a family tree
missing a branch.

*I hope she only hears
how despite it all,
she would be enough.*

GLIMMER

Beneath a sky
where the sun drips slow,
we gather close;
a flare unfurling across our skin.

Our daughter's giggle
ripples through the air.
I watch the light kiss her cheeks.
I like the way your hand rests on mine,
as if we are tracing a memory
we've carried all this time.

It's in these glimmers–
the hush between breaths,
the golden strands of morning
stretched across our faces,
that I find us whole.

It's not the vast moments of life,
but the gentle press of your presence.
Her sleepy smile.
The way the warmth nestles within us–
curling around each second,
holding us in gratitude.

These are the pieces that fill me,
small and fleeting, but together
they are *everything*.

Chocolate Chip Cookies

I can smell your freshly baked
chocolate chip cookies.
You always know what we need–
tender dissolves of comfort,
and letting our worries melt
into your embrace.

A Moment that Sings

The whistle of a kettle,
chopped wood crackling,
raindrops on the roof,
and a spoon's stirring tap.

I hear the drips and drops,
fingertips turning pages.
I hear the ticks and tocks
of time that had nowhere to be.

When life sings,
I try to listen.

Debbie A Radford

Cup of Coffee

You made me a cup of coffee.
I could smell the earthy scent
of hazelnut and thoughtfulness.

You gently hand me the mug,
wisps of warmth
rising like morning air.

Over the rim of the cup,
our eyes meet;
words aren't needed in this gesture.

You don't drink coffee,
and it's in this simple act,
I taste your deliberate devotion.

CAN YOU SEE IT?

Sparkles leap from the logs.
Embers flicker like fairies
in a candlelit ballet.

Our child nestled close–
a beautiful comfort in the glimmer.

In this glowing moment,
we find what was always there–
the magic we create
when we choose to see it.

Belonging

It's the way the room lights up
when they walk in,
or the way they know
what my eyes are saying
from a glance.

They can hear my voice
in a crowded room,
and know that wrinkle on my face,
before it's about to break.

It's the way they pull me in
when I'm chasing time.

It's the squeeze of a hand–
the embrace that receives me
for who I am.

I can float in that space–
where I don't have to prove,
just breathe;
just be,
knowing I'm entirely
enough.

POSSIBILITY'S PORTAL

Where reality bends and silhouettes play,
among the books and hearth's glow,
a threshold is hidden in the everyday–
a secret breathes through magic's seam.

A dance with time and space,
hints of otherworldly paths
in the ordinary's embrace.

Soft moments hint and hide;
a portal veiled
where dreams and waking collide.

Through the touch of worn wood grain,
just out of mortal sight,
sits a passage to a realm of arcane.

Imagination floats the in-between,
a pocket full of wishes,
and possibility not yet seen.

Cozy Whisper

In twilight's hush,
a murmur glides,
soft as night's breath–
like unhurried tides.

Candles glint
like warmth in the shade.
Shadows waltz–
ephemeral cascade.

The second swirls–
ethereal drift,
and around the heart,
is a tender lift.

Blankets cocoon
in a soft embrace;
understood secrets,
and unseen grace.

Quiet moments,
where dreams play–
a pause for troubles
with night's gentle sway.

Morning Magic

Soft golden joy spills
through the windows,
as chirping birds greet the dawn.

Rousing toes shuffle;
the scent of pancakes
wafts playfully through the air.

The table hums
with a gentle beckon,
inviting us to gather 'round.

It's morning magic—
a sunrise smile,
and all it takes
is for our eyes to open,
and welcome this new day.

Fairy-Touched

We sparkled,
our hearts kindled with wonder–
a glittering reflection,
and a pixie smile.

Worries dissolved
with an effervescence.

Joy bubbled and danced over our skin.

We had been touched by a fairy,
and granted the magic
of delicate enchantment.

WOODLAND WALKS

Our footsteps were cushioned
by emerald moss;
guided by illumed mushrooms
and winding fosse.

Chipmunks chattered cheerfully.
Stags and fawns
peeked shyly from the trees.
Squirrels settled their scampering,
as we walked with the forest breeze.

The earth felt alive
as our laughter danced–
like sunlight on the timbered floor.
The birds sang us a song and
flying wings fluttered evermore.

We built the fairies new homes
from twigs and leaves.
Wove crowns from white wood aster,
and pretended we were wooded royalty.

Our hearts were full of thicket thrill,
as we bid the forest a gentle farewell,
and twilight's sleepy hues
began to softly spill.

The Firefly

Tiny beacon in the night,
golden glowing,
delicate wings,
and shimmering light.

The firefly laces bliss
through our eager hands.
It gleamed like rekindled dreams.
in a hopeful land.

We had forgotten our wonder;
lost sight of the life that was living.
We were distracted from
the grief we had been given.

But it was in our firefly's gentle gift,
we revived the joy we once knew,
as gratitude and serenity
quietly renewed.

HOPE

It was in the candle's quivering clarity–
a reminder,
that even in darkness,
a small glint can guide us home.

Make-Believe

Sprinkle me in your fairy dust.
Let's dance like no one is watching.
Build turrets and castles
with pillows and blankets.
Let our giggles create swirls and eddies.

The sofa– our sailing ship.
The chair– our galloping horse.
The remote– a magical wand,
and bookcases are just
mystical mountains to climb.

There is no clock telling time.
So let's paint enchanted pictures
that take us to the places
we always wished to go.

In the world of make-believe,
it's often the place
we find the courage
to truly live.

My Favorite Season

We sat upon a blanket of burnished leaves,
the scent of slowing down
and my favorite season
sits on my nose.

Earth pours us a warm glass of daylight,
and kisses our cheek with a cool breeze.

I hear youthful laughter
running 'round trees,
chasing the squirrels
and a moment.

Foxgloves and sneezeweeds
sway in smiles–
drenching the air in dreams.

For a hum,
everything hushed,
and I could hear their heartbeats.

In this tick,
I know,
that if time chose to linger here,
my soul would have
found its peace.

From the Window Seat

Summer

We watched butterflies
trace paths across the sky,
and told stories from the lazy drift of clouds.
A pair of robins built a nest in the oak
and sang a sweet song.
We played with the sun's shadows
on the wooden floor,
and inhaled the scent of fullness.

Fall

You pointed to the falling leaves
and twirled with their dance.
A little black cat sprawled on the porch,
and we spotted a spider
spinning her web in glistening corners.
You wrinkled your nose
from cinnamon wafts,
and watched the fog roll in—
softening and releasing the earth.

Winter

As frost crept across the land,
we drew the patterns of snowflakes
and lacey imagination.

The fire crackled as
our toes found warmth in fuzzy socks.
Bare branches covered in snow
silhouetted the setting sun,
painting the sky in magenta and stillness.

Spring

After a long night,
the sunlight sparkled;
fresh raindrops clinging to the window.
We breathed in a burst of beginnings
and saw the first hints
of green shoot from the soil.
We watched sleepy life begin to wake,
and bobbed with a buzzing bee.

It was from the window seat,
we got to witness
the beauty of *change*.

Stardew

The sky spills with glitzy luster–
a silver rainfall, soft as breath.
Yet, it is his laughter,
and our daughter's tiny hands,
my shattered constellations were
stitched back into a whole heart.

When my universe unraveled,
and my courage threatened to
snap from its string,
I found in our shared breath,
a light more eternal
than those broken constellations.
I found a love so fierce,
it repaired what I thought
could never be whole again.

I realized it's not
the heavens that cradle me–
it's them.
The gentle weight
of her sleepy head on my chest,
his hand tracing soft circles on my back,
and that quiet magic we spin between us.

It's their stardew that fills
every broken corner,
until even the darkest fragments
gleam once more.

WANDER

We wandered where paths had no names,
beneath skies that held stories yet untold.
Her little feet tracing trails only she could see.
Where time curled and folded,
and we became travelers
in the dream of her youth.

We wandered with no map to guide us,
only the pull of wonder in her eyes.
She ran ahead, a wildflower in bloom,
leading us deeper into
the dance of leaves and lambency.

Together, we gathered moments like
fallen flecks of night,
and even the smallest speckles
became treasures in the grasp of her hand.

The world felt endless in her gaze.
Each step we took,
a new adventure unfolding.
Her fingers wrapped around ours,
tugging us toward the mystery
of every crooked trail.
And we followed, laughing,
because to wander with her
was to see everything
for the very first time.

Our Family

We are long legs
sprawling across the settee,
shrouded in blankets of warmth.

We are a scattered confetti of giggles,
and bedtime tales
that drift into dreams,
as the rhythm of snores begin.

We are the wild chorus of birdsong
echoing through the trees,
and the fireflies that dance
in time with the rustling leaves.

We are guitars strumming
moonlit melodies,
casting shadows that sway
like silver beeches
under starry ceilings.

Our hands are the keepers
of cherished promises.
Our eyes– silent sentinels whispering,
your tears are always welcome here.

We are the pages of poetry books,
the layers of earth's enigmas,
the resound of roads traveled,
and the musings of philosophers–

questions unfolding
into a multitude of answers.

Our family is the lingering scent of familiarity–
a closeness that can't be measured.

We are the dream
mingled in the breath of *I love you,*
and in the embrace of
unfiltered acceptance.

We are the heartbeat of
unconditional love.

Moonlit Magic

The night hums with possibility–
an effortless thread
spilling between the trees,
and if we dare to reach out,
the stars themselves will scatter
like pearls into our palms.

Magic is not hidden in ancient books,
but in the chances we take
when the world softens
in the ripple of our reflection;
where moonbeams
tell their secrets into our skin.

It's there, waiting,
in the crackle of dusk,
in the curve of our fingertips;
not bound by spells or chants,
but in the silent promise
we make to one another
to see the wonder in the ordinary–
to feel the pulse of magic
where our feet meet the earth.

Magic whispers,
reach for me.

Not with hands but with your heart.

And I watch as the moon
seeps its mysteries like syrup,
turning every shadow
into something that glows.

Magic was always here,
in the dust of forgotten corners,
in the stillness of moments
we almost let slip away–
waiting for us to look,
to name it,

to believe.

CHAPTER TWO

The Sunroom

Honey-Kissed

Every kiss you place on me
feels like a drop of honey.

A warm, golden,

melted,

    ooey,
      gooey,

smoothest,
      sweetest

    kind
    of
    kiss.

A honey kiss on my lips–
pure and lingering.
Something I could savor

           for a lifetime.

LOVE AT FIRST WORDS

I may have loved you at first sight,
but it was truly your first words—
the *hello* that tingled down my spine,
or how, *you look beautiful,*
made butterflies dance in my pit.
Your words, simple and sincere,
awakened my heart's slumber.

GENTLE RAIN

I'm falling for you like rain.
Not the fast and wild downpour,
but the gentle drizzle
while the sun is still out.

It's tender and soothing–
the kind of affection
I never knew I needed.

I glisten when you touch me.

I don't feel the need
to run and find cover.
It's the most natural thing–
letting myself dissolve
into the misty haze of your love.

WANDERING STARS

I spun in a tentative, fragile light.
A gentle shimmer of nascent dreams.
I was, perhaps,
the beginning of a glow,
and in my galaxy,
time moved in cautious steps.

But when I saw him,
time's turning hand halted.
Was it destiny?
A fated gravitational pull?
Because I saw him–
a drift in deep, steadiness.

He told me tales of his travels,
and described comets.
Before him, did I ever actually dream?
He was a fixed crave of knowledge,
and he wanted to show me the universe.

I always wondered
what happens when two stars
meet in a kismet kiss.
Now I know–
space explodes into understanding.
He and I,
we were always meant to find one another.

Summer Rain

My warm summer rain,
oh, how my skin soaks you in.

You drench me in those cool kisses,
and wrap around me like humid air.

I can't seem to breathe when I'm near you,
but yet, I feel so alive.

We are dancing puddles and
rumbles of thunder.

You touch me with reviving freedom,
Soak my hair in your laughter.
Paint my face with a glossy release,
because when I'm with you
nothing else matters.

Can we just stay
a moment longer,
before the sun
reclaims our reality?

JUST A KISS

I am dancing with the butterflies,
twirling under an open sky
as my bare feet patter with the earth.

With cheeks blushing,
and hair swirling,
I let this excitement
carry me across the land.

I daydream of forever
and a fluttery future.

I know,
it was just a kiss,
but I am so in love with you.

LOVESTRUCK

You're the breath caught in my throat–
a thought lingering long after the day fades.

I stumble over your name.
Each syllable a sweet ache,
and I'm lost in the sound.

Your smile is like a spell–
an enchanted pull I can't escape,
no matter how much I tug.

When you are not near,
my heart fumbles in the quiet you leave .

And your eyes are an earthquake,
shifting the ground beneath me–
a force beyond control.

Time stands still.
All that exists is us,
and the space between–
charged with unsaid words,
and a love that refuses to stay hidden.

FIRST LIGHT OF LOVE

What is a face familiar yet new,
and a smile that feels like home?

What is laughter that breaks
through the clouds,
or when eyes meet and pause the world?

What is anticipation that melts into ease,
or a soft promise unveiling itself
of something beautiful to come?

What is love at first sight,
but the warming hope
that maybe,
you have found your soulmate.

RIVER KISS

We drifted gently downstream on a river
carried by giant rose petals
while the sun painted the sky
in pastel shades,
and with the silkiest kiss,
you took my breath away.

My Fall

You are my fall–
a gentle, unhurried ease.
A coziness and intimate cuddle.
You are the comforting warmth
that I love to drink.
There is a deep vibrancy to you,
and I've fallen like the leaves.

YOUR EYES

Turquoise dreams
surrounded by sun-fire–
like I'm falling into the sky at sunset.
I could stay there forever,
but even eternity
wouldn't be long enough.

Dancing With You

Sunlight tumbles through the windows.
It paints the air with fragments
of our first melody.
Our bodies find one another,
feet and heartbeats in rhythm—
like no time has passed.

Sparkles dance off our cuddled fingertips.
The room becomes a canvas of our love—
tender brushstrokes and nostalgia.

It can be so easy to fall out of step.
Too often, we dance to different tunes.
But no music, my love, could ever compare
to the magic of dancing with you.

TRUST

Trust is so peculiar.
It's a warmth in your belly,
but an ache in your chest.
It's freeing yet fearful;
loyal and betraying.

It's a deep dive,
and a shallow collapse.

Trust can both love and devour all in one bite.

SHARED SILENCE

We've never listened more deeply
then in the silence
of our heartbeats dancing.

Like two hands
finding one another in the dark–
an understanding
that can't be spoken.

LET ME

Let me nestle into the spaces
you've left untouched–
a memory on the edge.
Let me slip a bit of wonder
beneath your skin,
until the ordinary
feels unfamiliar– electric.
Let me rest in the stillness
between your heartbeats,
where disbelief dissolves,
and hesitation hushes.
I'll arrive with the ease
of autumn's drift,
a quiet urging toward
what's always been waiting.
I'll brush against your doubts
like the air before a storm.
Let me scatter brightness
across your path,
each step gathering
a quiet thrill of fire in your chest.

Let me love you
                until you know it's magic.

Soulmate Sketch

If I could sketch you,
I'd carve each line
of your rooted calm
and steady resolve.

I'd drift into the sea of your gaze,
losing myself in your depth.

I'd trace
the rugged line of your beard,
brushing close each morning,
and your faint freckled marks–
a quiet map, just for me.

I'd capture the ease
held in your face,
the warmth of your smile–
an ember kindling something unspoken.

Yet how can a sketch reach the heart
of the one
who brings me home?

No line nor shade can go deep enough
to frame a love
this vast, this fierce.

SWEET NOTHINGS

I love sitting with you
in the afternoon sun;
my cheeks flushed from
the heat and your mischief.

Blushing and barefoot,
our feet and eyes graze
almost past the point of enticement.

Honey drips from your lips
as you whisper sweet nothings.

You love to feel me flutter,
and see my smile so smitten.

Will You Read My Story?

I hand you a book
bound in goodwill.
Tell you to read
until the moonlight fades;
until the weight of words
becomes too heavy to hold.

You trace the barked edges.
Gently turn them,
linger on certain confessions,
and smile at others.

You glance at me.
Sometimes with a
wince,
laugh,
or weep.

I've never let another venture this deep.
You say, *it's not finished.*
I say, *it probably never will be,*
and we just sit there,
amidst the sleuths of uncertainty, I ponder,
was it too much?

But you entwine your hand with mine,
and say something clever.
It was like the clouds breaking–
my story no longer bound by silence.

Stars

Like tonight and every night before,
you will eventually find me.

Whether it be quickly, slowly,
hesitantly,
or eagerly,

you will find me and hold me.

Whether it be passionately,
gently, or quietly,
your light will wrap around mine,
and we will glow.

No matter how far apart we rove,
We are destined to find one another
in the vastness of the sky,
for it was written in the stars.

Love is the Sun

Dawn

Love stirs in the warmth of a first breath—
tender blushes,
and gentle kisses in the sky.
The heart flutters awake.

Morning

Love bathes in the clement glow—
rising heat,
as energy stretches across the waking lands—
a golden wonderful embrace.

Noon

Love stands tall—
unyielding and bright.
A fierce and fiery blaze,
illuminating every corner of darkness.

Afternoon

Love is mellow—
soft and tender
in its gentle linger.
The heart is content.

Sunset

Love is a release;
painting and singing
in deep hues
of bowing breath.

Dusk

Love is quiet;
faded bustles
and purrs to soothe.

The heart is at peace.

A Garden of Love

Not all gardens grow in the open air–
some take root in hearts
long weathered by pain,
where every bloom of hope is a testament
to the hands that never gave up planting,
even in the depths of dormancy.

SCATTERED WISHES

The sun sketches
a calming song in the clouds.
Time hesitates to move beneath
the warming comfort.

Moony shadows swoop and
peek behind the lit corner,
just as the world is shifting and evolving,
and before the sunshine inhales
its last breath of day.
The golden beam
drips slowly
across the earth,
leaving traces
of what was,
and what could be.

The air thickens with the weight of
dream dust and desire.

A sweet softened glow captures
the moment before it slips away.
It writes the promise across our skin,
and we scatter our wishes into the sky,
hoping the moon
will mold them into
miracles.

STINGING TRUTHS

I look at you today
as though I've been given new eyes.

All the years and yesterdays
finally fade into forgiving cries.

It's true,
we are not the same;
not you,
not me.

Some days we are pitiless wasps,
some days we are gentle bees,
and the knowing will always be there,
that we both can cruelly sting.

And yet, in this moment as I gaze,
aware I would beg if need be,
for there is no universe
where you are not beside me.

Paint The Sky

Once, we painted skies, played sweet tunes,
now we're lost in endless afternoons.

Once, we danced to our own beat,
now it's dishes, bedtime, laundry, on repeat.

Notebooks blank, ideas confined,
passions left somewhere behind.

Books unread, aspirations pass by,
caught in life's perpetual sigh.
Days blend, weeks fade,
dreams on hold, stuck in the race.
It seems there's no time– no space.

Yet in this whirlwind,
you and I,
will one day again
paint the sky.

TABLE SET FOR TWO

I lay the table in silence,
each plate a quiet offering.
Exhaustion catches the air,
as if the weight between us
is too much
to speak aloud.

You sit across from me,
the space is filled with
what we've lost,
and I can feel
the stabbing of my sadness spilling over–
a quiet flood I cannot contain.

I try to shape a smile,
but it slips like water from my lips–
there's no use pretending
that this ache hasn't settled
in the marrow of me.

But you don't ask for joy.
You don't press
for the brightness I've buried deep.

Instead, your hand reaches,
steady and sure–
like a lifeline cast into the dark,
and I let you hold what's left of me.

There is no need for words.
You understand the gravity–
the quiet burn that has hollowed me out.

You allow me to sit here in my sorrow;
to wear the heaviness like a second skin,
without the need to wash it away.

Here, in this emptiness,
you make room for my breaking,
and in that quiet,
I find a strange kind of peace.
Not in healing, but in the permission
to remain undone
for a while longer.

My Light

When the earth shattered beneath my knees,
and my breath became a jagged plea,
you caught the fractured pieces.

As the world blurred
through a teardrop shroud,
you were the bedrock holding me
when I couldn't hold myself.

When I crumbled
like falling leaves on the ground,
you gathered me in your arms.

And in the silence
that followed my screams,
your hand found mine.

When the weight of loss
stripped me bare,
you covered me in courage.

When sorrow poured through me like rain,
you sheltered me with acceptance.

In the void that grief carved into my chest,
you planted a seed of light.
Your presence– a promise
that I would one day again
find my way back to life.

Love Notes

We trade love notes
in hints,
eyes,
fingers grazing,
a caress,
or a sigh.

We trade love notes
in the day,
in the night,
in the dark,
and in the light.

We trade love notes
off tongues
and kisses.
We speak in poems
and write in wishes.

Moss

Love me
slowly–
patiently.

Cling to the hidden parts of me,
softening what life has worn rough,
until I forget where I end
and you begin.

Love me like moss–
without rush or demand.
Turn the quiet spaces between us
into something tender– something alive.

Let your love cover me
even when I am weathered stone;
even when I can't feel the sun on my skin,
let your love cover me.

Grow where others would not linger.
Be the tenderness
I thought was beyond reach.

Love me like moss– persistent, kind,
always growing– always stretching.
A love that needs no grand gestures,
 just the soft,
constant presence
of *you.*

FOREVER YOUNG

We stumble through a kitchen waltz,
so I can fall into your arms again.
Your laughter is the tune
I never tire of.
You steal a kiss,
and I blush,
like the first taste of love.

You mock my jokes,
but your eyes say you'd endure them all
just to see me smile.
Hands find hands,
sparking something undimmed.
You chase, laughter tumbling,
and we hold time still.
Beneath the covers, we share secrets,
daring time to catch us.

In your gaze, a playful dare—
what are you going to do about it?
And with a wink,
the years fall away.
You tickle, I protest,
but neither of us wants to stop.
You give me that look—
the one that says, *you're mine*—
and it's as if we're young lovers,
discovering this feeling
for the very first time.

Fallen Star

She fell not with a crash, but a sigh,
as if the heavens exhaled
the secret it held–
love unspoken, and a spark too bright
to stay in the sky.

She tumbled through the velvet night.
A diamond tear slipped
from the eyes of infinity,
chasing the heartbeat it heard
in a whisp of wind.

In her descent,
she kissed the moon goodbye,
leaving behind a trail of golden joy,
and a love letter written
in the language of warmth.

The earth welcomed her with open arms;
caught her gently in a bed of soft grass,
as she nestled in the embrace
of the world that adored her.

Held by the earth's gentle hands,
the star shimmered with sweetness.
For in this love, she found a true home,
where falling was freedom,
and her burning became
the birth of eternity.

WHIMSY

It must have been that fluster of joy
tucked between shared glimpses–
a soft unraveling of
thoughts spoken without words.

As we spun beneath the moon,
feet barely touching the ground,
our hearts tangled in the glow
of forgotten rousing.

I thought,
perhaps, this is where forever forms–
in the spaces we leave for wonder.
In the way the world seems
to rearrange itself every time
you draw near.

How the earth tilts–
a soft, slow shift;
as though gravity itself has decided
to grant us a few extra moments
of weightlessness.

Labyrinth

You stepped into
the winding depths of me.
Where others saw only walls,
you found passageways.

Each turn–
a secret language.
Each curve–
a quiet dare.

Yet, you never faltered–
tracing the unseen
with an instinct
only you could hold.

My scrambled heartache,
you calmed with kindness,
bending the maze to your touch
until it no longer caged me,
but let me breathe.

Now, at its core,
I stand unguarded,
no longer alone–
because you knew the way all along.
I am the home
you've always belonged in,
and you have finally unlocked the door.

HALCYON

With steady hands and willing hearts,
we chose peace in a world
that thrives on wreckage.
We chose each other
when the winds urged us to drift away.

In the quiet of the forest, I took your hand,
and we carved calm from the chaos.
With our breaths as soft as morning mist,
we tethered ourselves to stillness,
tracing the edges of the moment–
like smoothing ripples on a placid lake–
undisturbed by the world waking.

We don't wait for the wilds to hush.
We quiet the woods with wordless warmth;
with a glance that says:
we are here,
together,
still.

You told me once
that love doesn't come as a gift
but as a creation,
and like today, and all days,
we are the makers.

CHAPTER THREE

The Bedroom

FIREPLACE

Will you light a fire for me once more?
We'll pile the wood.
I'll gather the tinder,
you the hope,
and we can kindle what embers are left.

Will you breathe life
into the ashes of our passion?

Set my heart ablaze—
burn the whole house down if you must.

Please,
I beg you.
Help me reawaken
the vigor of our love,
which we so desperately need
for our hearts to keep beating.

Phoenix Lovers

Never forget, my love,
we are phoenixes,
and this heartache
may crumble us to dust.

We may be singed and scorched–
turned to ashes.

We may burn.

But we will face these flames,
and rise anew
together.

LAID BARE

I was a late-November sapling,
stripped of its leaves,
laid bare for you.

You cradled my exposure
with a warming appreciation,
and a whisper in my ear–
you are more than enough.

UNDRESS ME

He doesn't rip off the clothes;
he melts away the weight of my fear,
gently revealing me–
like the sky at midnight,
surrendering only to the moon's soft light.

His touch slides like silk
over the rough edges of my memories,
smoothing the jagged places
until I am fluid in his hands–
free in a way I've never been.

With every motion,
he peels away the weight of old wounds,
not with force,
but like wind brushing over
the surface of still waters.
Until all that's left
is my bare reflection,
shimmering in his gaze.

His fingers trace scars
I've hidden like secrets,
yet he reads them as if
they were love letters penned by a heart
that only needed to feel safe
to tell its truth.

He undoes each button with quiet patience,
his fingers lingering on my skin,
learning the curves as though tracing a path
he was always meant to follow.

His hands slip beneath the fabric,
and I don't resist– I unfold,
as if I've been waiting my whole life
for these gentle winds
to stir the stillness inside me–
freeing an urge I never knew
was held so tight.

He pulls my hair gently to the side,
exposing the nape of my neck to the cool air,
and his warm exhale– a quiet surrender–
a release.

With every slow tug of my pants,
he's not just undressing me–
he's inviting me to let go of the layers
I've wrapped around myself–
pieces of who I thought I had to be
falling away.

His fingers glide along my back,
sliding beneath the surface like a soft breath.
He undresses not my body, but my soul,
and in the revealing,
I find my freedom.

BURNING CONNECTION

Let us forge a bond with our bodies,
one of feverish sweat,
burning with untamed flames.

In this heat, we abandon all restraint.
Our skin alight, crackling–
like embers in the dark.
The energy between us is primal,
a force that transcends flesh,
roaring with desire.
An inferno that consumes the night,
and leaves only our silhouettes
dancing on the walls.

We are bound not by words,
but by the spark of touch
igniting skin against skin.
Each caress an offering,
each breath a fan to the flame.

What we create here is molten–
a quiet eruption.
Not chaos but conception.
Our bodies become both flare and forge–
endlessly shaping, unshaping,
until we are nothing and everything
all at once;
fused in the quiet burn
of an eternal, restless glow.

ENTIRELY

I want you to
entwine your body in mine.
Wrap your arms around
my nakedness,
and love
all of me.

Desire

I am enchanted by you;
like a moth
endlessly drawn to a flame–
knowing the risk,
but craving the warmth.

SHAMELESS PLEASURE

How liberating it feels
to give my body permission
to discover its pleasures
without shame.

SMUT BOOKS

I'll read this part aloud to you.
A mischievous offering,
as I sultrily gaze into your unwitting.

You like to hear the words
spill from my lips–

thrust,
wet,
cock.

Giggles turn to gasps.
Warm bodies turn feverish.

Where were we?

Breath bristles your ear;
tongues tickle,
touch tangles.

I throw the book aside.
It was only to tease and tempt you.
I know *exactly* what to do.

FERAL

I don't want to be polite tonight—
no pleasantries or restraint.

I'm shedding my skin—
feeding a force that has been
smoldering for too long.

I drink unfiltered pulsing.
Feel it slide down my throat;
it tastes of lustful need—

consuming release.

I let my desires run feral.
I want you to taste the sharp edge
between my lips and
let the heat within me rage.

Watch Me

You watch
as I dance fervently
among the flames.

They burn hot
as sweat trickles down my arch.

You lick your lips
with rivetted longing.

As my hips dip and swing
with the rhythm of desire,
I swear I can hear
your heart
thump and pulse–

eager to consume something so lascivious.

GRIZZLY BEAR

Your quaking roar is my ecstasy.
Dig your claws into me.
Command me tall and untamed.
Devour me–
like I'm your feast after a long winter.
Ravish me in primal need.
Don't be coy,
I yearn for a love that is wild and unruly.

Good Morning

The morning swathes our bodies.
It's so revealing to be completely seen–
no darkness to hide in,
and yet, you embrace me.
Grab my thigh's dimples and
my skin's soft valleys,
kissing your way up
as the sun rises.

The sky ignites
as our warmth wallows and welters
on sweat-glistened skin.

We exhale
as the horizon hums
its quiet release.

It's gratifying,
affirming–
loving.

What a wonderful way
to begin the day.

Confessions

I confess,
I'm afraid if you see my wounds,
you'll think I'm beyond repair.
If you peel back my layers,
there won't be enough left to love.

I'm terrified
that the depth of my chaos
might drown you.

I confess
I'm afraid if I let you
see *all of me,*
there won't be any beauty left
in the bare truth—

I have been broken.

Bones

Will you still love me
when we are just
bones entangled–
no flesh to hide our truths,
only the hollowness of ribs and
the ivory sheen of our spirits?

GRIEVING

There seems to be nothing as intimate
as curling up in a ball of grief,
and letting you
wrap your comfort around me.

Velvet Touch

I ease into your respite–
soft and smooth;
a caress that soothes
the chipped surface of my armor.

Like velvet,
you blanket over me,
and I sink
into your plush protection.

My worries palliate–
a balmy kiss
calming my aching heart.

Your hand cupped my cheeks,
and my eyes reposed in knowing,

I could finally rest.

CREATION

We are the clay–
the soil cradling.

We are the song
the universe stirs
as it brings new life
into existence.

You kiss me
and the ground begins to open.
My fingers caress you
like a weaver on her loom.

We are the brush
dipped into creation.
Ripples of time–
colliding purpose.

We move as a gale force–
fated inevitability.

We are the pulse
ready to rupture.

Control is futile.
We are but vessels,
filled with the waters of fate,
flowing toward
what was always meant to be *ours*.

Stained Glass Woman

Our bodies are sacred places.
The vessels and scars
transcend light into an essence.

My frame is made up of crystal and enamel–
soldered with stretch marks and strength.

This body is colorful with
blemished beauty;
telling stories of existence.

Our bodies are healing spaces,
to light candles in,
and find peace.

MOTHER NATURE'S GIFT

I am carved in the image of abundance.
My curves– lush and bountiful
with earth's contours.
I am the embodiment
of Mother Nature's
generosity.

Seeker

You trace the silk of my moonlit river,
following each of my ripples
with a curved desire.
You trace each of my lines.
Brush the slopes of my vales,
and feel my lust rising.

Coax me in the cool breath of the open sea.

Caress me like a moonflower.
Open me under the stars.
Graze the misted window.
Follow my winding river–
curved, soft, and slow.

Map the terrain of my body.
Climb the peaks,
and glide on the hills.
Linger in the waves,
and wander the swells.

You are the seeker,
and I am the hidden world
that calls you
to discover me.

STILLNESS

In the stillness of the forest,
your touch breathes life into the quiet.
You are the subtle *whish* of wind
through my trees,
softly stirring with each pass.

There is no space between us.
You fill every part of me with

thick,
dense,
and
humid
air.

You settle on my skin.
Swirl around me,
soft and slow.
You are a lover's kiss lingering in the night,
and the keen yearning for *more*.

In the stillness of the forest,
my love,
your touch is the only sound
I need to hear.

Wild Pulse

Desire had never been so loud–
a roaring beneath skin.
The tremble of touch–
like thunder in silence.
Breathless currents
pulse through veins;
until the world burns
with the weight of wanting.

THE MUSIC BENEATH MY SKIN

I never knew my body could sing
until your hands became the instrument.
Each caress, a delicate note
strummed from my skin,
vibrating through my veins
like a melody born from longing.
Your fingers glide over me,
as though they've memorized
every chord that makes me hum;
every place that needs to be touched
to bring out the song I didn't know I held.
You play me softly at first,
coaxing my hidden music from its silence,
and soon, the melody swells,
rising and rising,
until I am no longer contained–
releasing a crescendo so raw and powerful,
it rings out,
like the highest note of a symphony.
I tremble on the edge of a near scream,
until the final chord is released–
a shuddering sigh
that leaves me both undone and fulfilled.
As silence swathes over us like a dull,
lingering harmony,
I can still feel the energy
beneath my skin,
until we play the song again.

HONEY

Honey pools in the dip of my waist.
It flows like warm sunlight down my thighs.
Every curve a golden river,
every step a supple pour.

Like a honeycomb,
my body is textured and endless,
mailable like bees wax,
with threads of dripping sweetness
curling around my hips.

My skin gleams like amber
in the late afternoon–
something one cannot help but savor.

I wear the curves of my body
like sugar silk–
soft, lustrous, and shimmering
in a sunshine touch.

I am the sap of my creation,
overflowing in luxury.
I melt into the depths of my form,
as smooth as nectar's fall– slow and sure.
Each layer of me ripened in richness,
and oozing in flavor.

ABUNDANT BODY

She carries the moon's fullness–
curves like a silken night,
swathing the sky's freckles.

She is rolling hills
and fertile valleys–
rich with taste and glut.

She is the swell of the ocean–
undulating with the surf of the tides–
a rise of waves
one wishes to ride.

She is harvest–
ripe fruit and
a garden's bounty.

She is the mountains–
cradling the clouds
in her arched peaks.

She is a masterpiece–
a body sculpted
by the hands of
earth's lavish need
for magnificence.

HINTERLAND

Take my hand and let us drift
where the maps falter–
past the edge of knowing.

We'll find ourselves in that unmarked sky,
where night jewels pulse–
unseen, but felt beneath the skin.

There's a country beyond
where your breath on my neck is the wind.
Where we abandon certainty;
trade it for an alluring throb,
and creeping goosebumps.

I want you in the spaces
between my unknown;
slipping,
melting,
dissolving.

I want to wander with you
where no paths lie.
Where the grasses of my dreams
meet the rivers of your ache.

In the hinterland of us,
I want to lose the compass
and feel only your fingers tracing the way.

Swimming in Starlight

We float where the trees kiss the sky,
being held by liquid gravity and lust.

Moonlight bends around us.
I am lost in the way
your body strokes the ripples
of my skin.

Shimmers
and shivers
slowly suspend
down my spine.

I spiral at the touch.
I curl my legs around your hips
and sink.

Hold me here forever.
Fill me with starlight
until I am nothing,
but a breath on water,
dissolving into you.

Ivy

Ivy, soft and silent,
seeks a slow twist
through untouched stone,
curling in undiscovered spaces.

Each vine speaks without sound,
burrowing itself in all
the corners and crevices.
Pressing gently against sensitive walls—
its grip like a breath drawn close.

No force,
only a tender persistence.
An embrace
that wraps around curiosity,
finding space
where light barely reaches,
and holds,
not to tether,
but to belong.

Free to Feel

Let yourself rise,
surefire and unruly–
a pulse that breaks the chains
you've placed upon yourself.

Kiss the flame.
Lick the edges of your hesitation.
Dare yourself to feel the rapture
you've long denied.

Let your skin thrum–
like earth after rain.

Soak in every pleasure your body offers you.

Let your fingers explore–
dawdle, glide, and graze.
Wander where there was once restraint.

Untangle the shame–
sway, savor, and
sing to arousal's siren song.

Dissolve the weight of guilt.
For you are the swelter, the tempo,
the pulse of pleasure itself–
unfolding into your own hands,
and free to feel
without apology.

CHAPTER FOUR

The Nursery

Our First Breath

They nestled you gently against my heart,
where the beating of our souls
met for the first time.

Your eyes, like pillowed clouds
over the amber leaves
of dreamwood trees,
held a soft invitation,
drawing me toward a world
awakening with wonder.

In that sacred moment,
we breathed our first breath–
a tender sigh that echoed through the sky,
binding us in a story
written by
the hand of fate.

TINY BUTTERFLY

Tiny butterfly,
fluttering through the day,
learning to stretch your wings,
and moving with the sways.

Flit and fly,
princess of the sky.
Perch upon the petals.
Rise until your soaring settles.

Catch the colors of curiosity,
smell the scents of surprise.
Feel the enchanted earth
each time you close your eyes.

Tiny butterfly,
all I ask of you
is to capture the world.
Let your wings of wonder
freely unfurl.

A Wish That Dared to Hope

She carries within her a wild wish.
She buries it in the earth,
breathes into the brushwood,
and sings to the soil.

What are miracles
but a hope that dared to wish?

Beneath her ribs,
a star stirs.
Her belly beams with brilliance
from the glistening sun.

A heartbeat awakens
that slumber of time,
and her spirit crafts a life
from dust and dreams.

What are miracles,
but a wish that dared to hope?

So, I dare to hope
this wish will become a

miracle.

One Daughter

When someone asks me
how many children I have,
I want to say,
one on earth and a few in the sky.
I want to say,
my heart has loved
many things it never knew.

I want to just   cry.

I watch from afar
as happiness blooms
third and fifth times
for so many gardens.

I shamefully linger
like an envious snake
salivating at the beauty.

I hide beneath the grass
as heavy voices
yell out to be grateful
I even have
a sliver of light.

It hurts to be desirous.
It's painful to be lost in wanting.

Yet, I swallow that sadness,
and simply say,
I have one daughter,
but we are trying.

Fairy Wings and a Tutu

Through her eyes,
we were not in the living room.
We were in the enchanted forest,
skipping with unicorns,
bunnies, and squirrels.

I don't know if she knew
how sad I had been–
on the brink of letting darkness
swallow me whole.

But there was something too enticing
about the request to follow her
into a wooded dreamland.

I don't know if she knew
how badly I needed to pretend;
how desperately I needed
just a moment of *magic.*

SUMMERTIME HAPPINESS

You were my summertime happiness–
the soft hum of bees in a blooming garden–
a chime of the flourishing life
you would've been.

I ache in the yearning and the grief.
If only,
we were given the chance
to meet.

STOLLEN SUNSHINE

When the sunshine
has been stolen from your womb,
even just once,
you'll never be able to experience
the joy of the sun the same again.

It will be radiating within you,
but you'll always be

waiting,
anticipating,
expecting

to wake up
to an empty sky.

LAVENDER LULLABY

When the world whirls too wildly
I wrap myself in a lavender lullaby.
It whirs and whispers,
softly smoothing
the wrinkles of my worried mind.

NATURAL BEAUTY

She is a vision–
like dappled sunlight
peeking through the leaves
of a blooming lilac tree.

It's a natural beauty–
like wind dancing in hair,
butterflies singing to flowers,
clouds painting pictures,
a storm's rainbow.

She is simple,
but astonishing.

She is gentle.
She is kind.

I look towards her sunset smile;
breathe in her misty laughter.

She calls to me now
to take her hand and
come run wild in her
dreamland of wonder.

I take her hand,
and I don't look back.

MOTHER SUN

The sun– perhaps a mother after all,
for she breathes her warmth into the soil,
a quiet, golden flood spilling over the earth,
giving without asking.

She rises, an ancient song stitched in light,
holding every seed, every branch
in the reach of her glow,
a silent embrace across fields and mountains.

Surely, she holds a heart alight,
its pulse a steady keeper of the hours,
a vow that darkness is only a passing thing.

The sun must know the secrets of healing,
for her touch smooths and mends
in ways no other light can.

Arms of gold stretch wide,
and each dawn, she murmurs of home,
her gentle gaze guiding us
back to where we belong.

My Rainbow Girl

When you ask her,
she says her favorite color
is rainbow.

It's fitting because,
she will find the magic
in every hue of life.

Like the color of kindness–
a warm golden glow.
No matter who it is,
she gives them her honied hello.

She never hesitates
to spread her tangerine glee–
silly, wild, and absolutely free.

You'll feel her heart
in lavender love
showing up
in her gentle, soothing hugs.

And I just adore
the adventure in her guise–
a curious green
and a spirit growing to the sky.

Even her tears
still show the light.
Her eyes find stars
even on the darkest of nights.

Every day,
she shows me new colors
in the world.
She is my vibrant,
beautiful,
rainbow girl.

HOLDING ON

Exhausted
in a world
that won't rest.
I hold onto my child,
like a wilting flower
clinging to the last rays of the sun.

TENDER

The young tree leans toward the elder,
offering life to its fading limbs.
Once proud and tall,
the elder bows low,
its brittle branches
weighed with quiet shame.

Dry leaves crumble at its feet,
a reminder of the strength that once was,
now lost in the wind.

The elder shifts in silence,
unable to stand as it once did,
ashamed to seek the shelter
of her young one's shade.

Beneath the surface,
their roots meet softly,
as the elder trembles,
holding back the ache of needing care.

And though sorrow clings to the bark,
the young tree stands firm,
teaching the elder
that even in weakness,
there is dignity
in being held.

SUNFLOWER

In the womb of the earth,
there is a sunflower.
Her sun-seeking face
stretches towards the sky.

She sways to the pulse of heartbeats.

Her center nurtures
sprouting promises,
and nesting dreams.

Come autumn, this sunflower will flourish.

She will carry and nourish her blossoms,
then put them back
into the earth
to grow.

This is birth.
This is being a mother.

Moonlit Lullaby

The moon spills silver
through the trees,
as shadows dance
in midnight's breeze.

Footsteps trace
the forest's
gentle hum,
with sleepy eyes
and visions
yet to come.

In the wild embrace
of whistling pines,
we find a thrum
in the rustling leaves–
a lullaby where
the forest dreams,
and perhaps
so can we.

LITTLE QUEEN

The power lies within
our radiant sunshine.

She is made of energy
that enlightens
and ignites.

She is the sky's songbird
whose voice brightens
cloudy sadness.

Her ember eyes end wars.
Her embrace unifies enemies.

Perhaps she has just taken
her initial steps around the sun–
still in the dewy morning of her reign.
But she
was made
to rule kingdoms.

Long live our little queen.

GLITTER

You are glitter–
a sparkling dust
that brings life
to my dullness.

How do you do that–
shimmer my world
with just a smile?

Rest

I let myself sit tonight.
My mind had been tossing in angst all day.
I needed to let the comfort of stillness
wrap around me like a blanket.
My heart muffled my mind,
and gently breathed,

it's okay to rest.

Happy Flowers

I try and look for the cheerful flowers–
the sunflowers, daisies, and tulips.

I try to paint their shades on my heart–
golden, lemon, and butter.

I really am trying to be happy.

But sometimes,
all the colors
and scents
of happiness,
only make me
more sad,

because there is
no replacement for

                    you.

LITTLE JUST A WHILE LONGER

Will you let her be little just a while longer?
Let her play and pretend
that the world she imagines
won't take from her
before anything is given.

Allow time to slow and lengthen,
so she can be a dreamer,
and dance without fear.

Will you let her be little just a while longer?

UNDER THE COZY SKY

Come, sit with me,
my little moonbeam,
and I'll rock you sweet to sleep.

I'll gently sweep
the curls from your face
and tickle your tiny feet.

We'll sing
a tired lullaby
and I'll whisper
love notes into your ear.

Come, rest with me,
my little sun star;
in my embrace
you have nothing to fear.

Sunless Room

A sunless room?
Oh no,
it will not do.

The walls and our spark
drained of joy–

colorless,
drab,
and dour?

Who lost their sense of humor?

We open the curtains.
Let the laughter spill and swirl,
like a babbling breeze.

Flick the light's paintbrush
and roll around senseless.

Let's be mad with giggles.
Slap a knee and spit out our drinks.
Smile so wide,
that the world falls into our happy mouths.

I will splatter this sunless room;
pour and splash the walls
with all the hues of
your silly sunshine.

STARLIGHT PRAYERS

As we lay beneath the midnight sky,
my daughter asks me about prayer–
her small voice blending
with the yawning world.

We spoke of God
under a blanket of constellations,
her innocent wonder
illuminating the darkness–
like a newborn moon.

She asked, *why do people pray?*
I spoke of my prayers to God–
wishes, hope, and faith.

We spoke of loss, heaven, angels, and saints.
She imagined babies with wings,
flitting among the fairies;
their presence, warm and comforting,
even though unseen.

We lay there, the cool grass beneath us;
midnight keeping our secrets,
as she believed our unborn souls
had become heavenly guardians,
always near.

She saw them as beings of light,
playing with the stars;
that they were real, and always will be.

Magic Mother

My mother swirled rainbows
through the mist,
and laid them gently
at my door.

She clutched my heart and told me,
the light is coming soon.

My mother, with her magical wand
carved diamonds into the night sky
to show me the way to faith–
to believe the magic is coming;
to hold on just a while longer.

PURPOSE

She chases the world
with wide-eyed wonder.
Uncovers buried magic
and lifts it to the surface.
She brightens a hopeful light within me;
the blue flames dimming.
My empty spaces fill with purpose.

Her awe–
it was that hand reaching back in time,
pulling me out of the anguish,
and into the light of day–
mending the cracks
in my forgotten joy.

Spirit of the Forest

We paint our sage and umber wishes
beneath the songleaf sycamore–
singing with the nightingales
and rustling winds.

I love to place flowers in your hair,
as our laughter rumbles under twilight skies;
adorning our eyes with the glow of fireflies.

I love it when we swim
like mermaids in crystal streams.
How we watch the woodland creatures
in their hidden burrows–
writing tales of their daydreams.

I hold onto our midnight cuddles,
listening to the owls' gentle lullabies.
I paint our stories in the air,
not to capture you,
but to reflect your wonder–
to hold the quiet magic surrounding you.

Because you, just as you are,
is the spirit of the forest–
enchanted and *alive*.

MOTHERS

With a glance, she commands the wild–
like light from shadow–
peace from storms.

Her hands create worlds–
mending what's unseen.
She is a quiet force that shapes
the very air we breathe.

NIGHT'S SOFT CRADLE

Dusk braids itself through pine-needle lace,
as roots curl in whispers, weaving shadows' trace.
Elder birches cradle stories in bark-bound skins,
where moss-wrapped secrets deepen within.

Mushrooms glow, a quiet, pulsing light,
while crickets hum low, summoning night.
Tiny moths drift on moonlit streams,
gathering near where the forest gleams.

Beneath willow's watch, dreams slip and sway,
in moon-dappled folds where children lay.
Stars bloom above like forest-born flowers,
lulling little eyes through quiet hours.

DAISY

I dream you Daisy–
a bloom that rises from the soil of my heart;
born from all the tears
I've watered the earth with,
waiting for you.

I plant your name, Daisy,
with trembling hands–
an offering of hope
that one day,
we will dance
in the winds of my longing.

I've loved you before you grew, Daisy;
a wish spun from stars,
rooted in faith that
one day,
I will hold you close
and feel the warmth of the sun again.

You are my prayer–
the heartbeat I hear in silence.

So, I wait for you, Daisy
in delicate dreams,
until you rise from the shadows of sleep
and find your place
in my arms.

QUEENS OF THE DEEP BLUE

Close your eyes and imagine,
beneath the lagoon's shimmering veil,
we slip into a world unseen;
where light dances in a wavy cadence,
and our breath weaves the currents
into threads of wonder.

We swim through
forests of seaweed
as the fish giggle in riddles,
and we slowly become
wrapped in tidal reveries.

With each plunge, we imagine
the glistening sea as a gateway
to a hidden kingdom,
where only the brave dare to go.

The sun's rays turn to streams of gold,
guiding us deeper into caves
where treasure chests of curiosity
wait to be found.

And as we inhale this deep blue imagination,
we discover a realm filled
with mangrove magic
only we can see
and we are
its queens.

DEWDROP

Each moment clings to my skin,
until I find myself
soaked in my dewdrop's sweetness.

I gather the tiny,
fleeting speckles
in my hands.

Her laughter,
the grasp of my pinky,
the sound of soft breathing,
sparkling eyes of wonder,
messy curls falling upon her face,
a titled head,
and a smile drenched in sunlight.

I close my eyes,
let the droplets fall upon my cheeks–
every kiss,
every cry.
I bask in her gentle sprinkles.

I drink in
every
last
drop
until the vastness of her love
carries me away.

Lily

You are the light that flickers
before the sun rises—
a quiet warmth that fills the air—
gentle, yet enduring.

You ask questions like breaths—
each one pulling the world closer,
as if it were waiting for you to find it.

Your kindness is a bastion—
steady and sure.
It's the way you touch life;
how you move
through the smallest of moments.

I watch as your laughter breaks the silence—
turning stillness into something that dances.

Every time you twirl beneath the sky,
the clouds take a breath,
as if they've just remembered
what it feels like to be hopeful again.

When you sing,
it feels like the earth listens,
and in your sway,
time forgets to pass.

You hold everything in your hands
without even knowing it,
and I feel the weight of the world lift
when you're near.

Hope rests in the way you see the world–
not in grand gestures
but in the smallest glimpses–
a quiet belief that love
will always find its way through.

You are beauty–
catching the world in your eyes,
and carrying all the love

I'll ever need.

CHAPTER FIVE

The Library

THE SECRET HIDEAWAY

I meet them in the secret hideaway,
my spirit sisters.
We carved out an oak tree trunk,
and made a space
in which was safe to share
dreams and tears within.

As we step through the gnarled bark,
the demands and pressures
release from our chests–
like souls returning to the sky.

Soft beams of sunlight filter through
as worries fade away.
Feet meet steps
leading to a bright basin,
and we bathe in our stories
and confessions.

I never knew such a place could exist–
a place to be truly seen.

SURRENDER

There's a release
in letting the leaves fall,
like loosening the knot around a heart
that was never meant to be tied.

The woods have a way of remembering,
as if every branch looks back at its break—
each scar, a story written in the bark.

In the quiet surrender of autumn,
the branches shed without regret,
trusting the wind to carry
what no longer serves them,
as if loss itself could be a kind of grace.

It's in this stillness,
I understand—
there's a beautiful freedom
in just letting it all go,
I find myself disentangled,
branches bare,
belonging only
to the boundless sky.

Day Dreaming

A gentle breeze releases its grasp–
letting worries drift like fading breath.

In the mind's deep hush,
I am seen–
a glow of understanding,
pure as a spider's web.

As I trace the filaments,
patterns of truth are awakened,
spun from the silk threads
of sunlit dreams;
where I dance on poetry lines,
paint the sky in starlight,
make wishes,
and they come true.

I don't sleep,
I daydream.

Sleeplessly,
I fantasize with open eyes.

APPETIZING

People say I'm not as soft and tender
as I used to be–
they miss my appeasing flavor,
because it felt comforting for them
to indulge without judgment.

I grew tired of the gluttony
and realized life is much more savory
when kindness is a shared meal.

FAREWELL

Not every character
gets to make it
to the sequel
of my story.

Some fade into the footnotes,
lost in the quiet spaces
where words no longer reach.
They linger in the margins,
ghosts of a tale
that once was.

I must turn the page,
be open to the unseen,
where unfamiliar voices rumble
with wild potential,
and each chapter pulses
with the thrill of unwritten lines.

MISUNDERSTOOD

Some people will never understand you.

While you're trying to show them
your moon,
they are only interested in your sun.

They'll scan the sky for your stars
while missing the universe
in your eyes.

You're painting with colors
not yet invented–
and they can only see
in black and white.

They'll watch
as you plant seeds in your garden,
but they will never be able to
appreciate what blooms.

Some people will never understand you–
that you're the bird soaring in the sky.

All they will ever see
is an escape,
and not the
freedom.

It's Not Me, It's You

It's not you, it's me,
I'd weep to the trees,
as if the forest cared to hear
my haunted apologies.

It's not you, it's me,
a mantra for the night,
I feared the darkness in your eyes
more than the absence of my light.

It's not you, it's me,
I'd bend to calm the storm,
while shadows circled, grumbling
that silence was the norm.

But what if,
just what if,
it's not me,
it's you?

The moon unveiled a bitter truth,
the cedar no longer lied,
you cast the spell that dimmed my spark,
but now the flames won't hide.

In these revealing woods, I stand,
no longer bound or small–
it's not me who ever fell,
it was you who made me crawl.

I Thought About It

Like a breeze hesitating at the window,
I thought about reaching out to you.
I want to call your name.
It aches too much
having so much to sing
while your ears are only open
for a brief song;
as effervescent as a passing breath.

Am I asking for too much?

It's strange because
I could listen to your stories all day.
I wouldn't mind your tales
of skyward journeys and hidden nests.
I would truly cherish hearing
about another one of your flights
through the treetops,
basking in the sunlight.
Truthfully,
it hurts that it's never my branches
you return to.

Did you know
I've stood tall through many seasons
just to be near you.
When I say I love you, it's deep–
as if my roots twist intently
just to grow and see you.

Yet you can't even perch beside me
beneath the same star-studded sky.

I think I'll always be your little sapling,
despite how much I've grown.
I don't doubt you'll keep leaving me
with fleeting feathers and shallow songs,
but if you truly knew me,
you'd know that a lasting presence
is worth so much more.

It hurts to yearn for an empty branch.

You may never choose me on your journey;
perhaps you'll always see me small
in your vast, towering world.

I thought about calling you,
even sending a message carried on the wind.

I truly did.

But I think it would have just been
another leaf falling unnoticed–
lost in your endless sky.

GROWING APART

People grow apart.
Their tangled vines slowly loosen over time
and unravel from the link.

Once an entwined connection,
now softly frays,
seeking separate sunlight in a split dawn.

We find new paths,
move in different directions.

I no longer recall the little things about you.
I find myself on the outside–
an observer,
just looking in.

There is only dullness
where colors used to beam.
I can feel the empty space
where there used to be closeness.

I'll call you back turns into *I forgot.*
We should make a plan,
but it feels more like an imposition.

Sturdy bonds begin to wilt.
Roots, deep and unseen,
just twist in hollow soil.

It's simply a surface
of where we used to stand.

I could cling to the splintered brittles—
give it time to rebuild.
But we both know,
this is better left buried
under wistful light.

HANGING BY A THREAD

It began with
an exhausting tension–
petty, passive-aggressiveness,
framed in a friendly
half-hearted laughter.

I started not to like you.

I held onto time,
like you can't just pour out the cup
and start over.

I sat with half-filled amity for years,
scared to be lonely
only to realize,
feigning happiness
created my solitude.

You drink from every cup, yet never pour.
You're the hand that reaches but never extends.

And over time, fibers that once may have
held together a twisting of connection,
weakened and now sway precariously,
leaving behind a completely frayed bond.

I was wrong to have pretended
I could have forgiven you–
to believe a ripping rope
could just happily become undone.

I told you I wish you well,
and I meant it.

But in severing the final thread to you,
the loom of beginnings
began to weave anew,

and I could finally let out
a breath of
              relief.

Twilight

There are moments like twilight–
a dusky embrace of day and night,
where the moon whispers
a secret to the fading sun's glow,
and in that quiet, I finally know,
there is peace found
in letting go.

BURN

You could set every part of yourself on fire.
You could smolder
into embers
for easiness of others.
You could reduce your flame to a flicker,
but even then,
some will say your fire is still
too bright,
too wild,
too free.

But the sun,
it never dims on behalf of closed eyes.
It rises–
it burns,
because the world needs its fire.

So let your flame roar,
surge higher.

For those who fear it
were never meant
to stand in your warmth.

Love Letter

She wrote herself a love letter.

Penned it with scribbles of affection
on delicate paper and etched with
honied fondness.

She sealed her letter in warm wax,
and then accepted it

unconditionally.

SHADOW FRIENDS

In the deepest folds of night,
when the world's weight smothered itself
across my shoulders,
I will remember those who chose
to stand with me in the shadows.

They asked for nothing–
not a word,
nor a tear.
Not a reason,
nor a promise.

They didn't demand that I rise or shine–
didn't pull me toward the light
I wasn't ready to face.

They simply existed.
Their quiet presence– a balm.
Their silence–a refuge.

These were the ones who knew
that in the heart of darkness,
sometimes the greatest gift
is the grace
to be still,
to simply breathe,
and to feel the steady pulse
of another's heart
beside your own.

Shooting Star

I always remember the day you told me
about seeing a shooting star.
You were sitting on the sandy beach
of the emerald coast
under a full moon.

You had said,
I asked the universe for a sign,
and it sent me a shooting star.

We spent the next year
talking of our dreams and wishes–
speaking them into existence.

And as the days and months went on,
we also spoke of our fears and doubts;
how they can sometimes feel
like diving deep into a dark ocean,
and there would be no light to cling to,
but we dove in anyway.

I know that without you,
I would have never jumped.
I would have never dreamed that big.

And when my feet plunged
into the inky unknown,
there you were,
like sky-fire,

glowing with beautiful magic.

You are the light I cling to
when my heart doesn't know the way.

I too asked the universe for a sign,
and it nudged me towards you,
my own shooting star.

Raison d'être

I could go down hundreds of different paths.
Take a turn here,
and there.

I could be a lot of different things.

But there is one dream,
one path
that makes my heart beat.

It is my raison d'être.

STORIES

I fall in love with
raindrops drumming gently;
the concrete wearing
a petrichor scent.

Coffee breathes richly,
and book pages rustle.

In this quiet corner of peace,
I settle like a gentle fog;
embracing warm sips and stories
that invite me into
lives yet to be lived,
and hearts yet to be loved.

Pan, Play me a Song

Under the shade of a sprawling ancient oak,
there is the singing and laughter of nymphs.
Their voices mingle with
Pan's musing melodies.

Lilies and blushing geraniums sway
with the dancing of their unbridled feet.

Love and joy are teeming,
because here, in this meadow,
we are all allowed to be free.

Hanging with Dionysus

Take me to the seaside mountains,
where we can dance
with the satyrs and snakes,
and tell stories about being misunderstood.

You can feed me your grapes and
fill me with pomegranate bliss,
then we'll run wild between
the trees and vines
that dare to hold us back.

I just want one day of your chaos—
to know what it feels like to
get lost in the madness of living.

Soul Sister

We run wild in the forest;
loose dresses and bare feet
gliding over moss-covered trunks
as myrtle buds brush our spirits.

We are free and fierce–

unyielding to the constraints
of roles and expectations.

We are women. We are hunters of thrill;
swimmers and survivors.

We have faced the boar of impossibility;
clutched its tusks and
ripped out its sneering heart.

We dance and feast upon doubt.
We laugh and sing under wishful gleams.

No one will understand us,
but we understand–

the smell of earth and dreams;
the sound of streams waiting to carry us
to the place our souls desire.

Let's run some more, my sister–
life's possibility awaits us.

HANDRAIL

You were my handrail
as I climbed this staircase.
I clutched onto your sturdy frame
as you whispered,

I won't let you fall.

The Poets, My Friends

Enchanted by wild spirits,
like rivers rushing
through tangled thoughts,
their emotions root deep as an elder,
branching in daydreams from river mist.

In shadowed groves, thoughts grow thick,
and in their stillness,
they hear the quiet language of words.
Verses lush as forest floors,
they scatter words like seeds,
letting them grip the earth
in the fertile soil of the soul.

In spaces between lines, I wander,
lost and found in the dance of their pen,
where chaos hums with harmony.

In their worlds of woodsmoke and whispers,
I become infinite,
a traveler of wonder,
forever in love
with the poets.

SWEETIE

How courageous you are,
to walk in a gluttonous world,
and share your sweetness with it.

Like nectar
dripping from bluebells,
you offer your light
without reserve,
even as the world
takes more than it gives.

Your kindness lingers
like sugar on the tongue,
soft as spun candy,
filling the air with
the scent
of something sensitive.

And even when
the world
is spoiled,
not deserving,
you still believe
kindness
belongs to all.

LAUGHTER

I laughed freely once again,
like shattering a glass cage
with the pure resonance of joy.
Each giggle, a shimmering note
reverberating through the silence
that once held me captive.

It's as if the darkness has cracked open,
releasing a flood of hope
that dances in my chest,
scattering doubt
with every echoing peal.

The laughter rises like a firebird
from the ashes of sadness–
a fierce and radiant reminder,
that even in the deepest abyss,
the essence of joy
was merely waiting
to be reborn.

GUARDIAN

There are those who love
with magic seeping from unseen springs–
compassion flowing without end.

They find you in the storm,
wrap their light around your darkness,
and pull you back from the edges.

They are rare,
timeless,
unfading–
with warmth igniting the skyline.

Sometimes you wonder
if they stepped out
from your deepest dream,
and if grace allows,
you'll get to offer them
your own light in return.

Friendship

When the world grows dim,
I'll steal a shard of moonlight
and let it linger for you,
wrap wishes in wildflower hues
and scatter them like seeds in the wind.

I will offer you the shade of a maple,
and foxfire to illuminate your way
back to joy's meadow.
We will trace constellations
in one another's skies,
and sing duets with the crepuscule birds,
until the night sways with our song.

When waves rise fierce,
I'll hand you my compass,
chart a course through chaos,
and throw the truths of our souls
to dance among the storm.
Let us twirl beneath rain-soaked skies,
chasing the lingering dusk
with lanterns carved from hope.
I'll weave the flowers of your laughter
into a crown, asking you
to wear your smile unbroken.

In this bond,
there will always be a flame
to kindle our dreams–

just look towards my light.

THE FOX AND THE FROG

The fox, with leaves clinging to its fur,
steps into the clearing
where the frog rests in the shade.

No words pass,
no movements beg to be made.
The air thrums between them,
charged, yet unspoken–
a shared space
that never needs explaining.

As the fox sinks into the ground,
as rough as the landscape,
the frog watches with easeful knowing:

no one is polished,
no one is perfect,
and that is where they meet–
where everything melts away.

In that raw,
untouched repose,
they find not just enough,
but the purest sense of acceptance–
of *friendship.*

REWRITTEN

In pages not my own,
I uncovered pieces
I didn't know were missing.

Ink seeped into forgotten spaces,
etching a thousand lives into my skin.

Each word, a chisel—
shaping my reflection,
their strength becoming mine.

I wandered their worlds,
lost and found,
their endings sparking new beginnings,
until their voices taught me
how to hear my own.

Aᴇʟɪɴ Aѕʜʀʏᴠᴇʀ Wʜɪᴛᴇᴛʜᴏʀɴ Gᴀʟᴀᴛʜʏɴɪᴜѕ

She rose from the ashes to ignite–
a storm of flame and steel
commanding with unmatched ferocity.

A relentless spirit;
her wild roar echoing through the world.

It was in her fire-forged soul,
I found the strength of resilience.
Her unyielding nature– a provocation
to no longer cower.

She clawed,
ripped,
wailed,
and exploded
into a force of resolve.

She burned brighter than a thousand suns,
blazing in defiance
of anyone who dared to doubt.

It's in her fireheart that I know
courage is a flame that cannot be extinguished;
and when the world seeks to shatter you,
become the force that remakes it.

The Wolf

You are striking.
Warm pools of soil dipped in syrup
swirling in your eyes;
grit cutting at the jaw.

You are the wolf;
and wolves can sometimes be
misunderstood.

They are the hero and villain;
slayer and slain;
hunter and hunted.

You tell me
you often feel people only love you
when they need you.

But I see you for who you are–
rugged and untamed,
carrying the song of the moon within you.

A spirit forged in nightfire's strength;
you are beautiful,
like love itself said,
this world needs you.

Your loyalty runs through the earth,
like mycelium beneath the forest floor.

You are the wind between towering pines,
sunlight that caresses a cheek.

And when you clutch me in your embrace,
I wonder,
who could ever hurt something so nurturing?

I see you—
when you run towards
the flinching darkness;
clawing the unknown,
only to share the light you find.

You silhouette the nocturnal sky,
and guard the rising sun.
You are the wolf;
and I see you.

Book Magic

It is not an escape, but an encounter.

I've explored many worlds,
and felt endless love.
I've seen the beginning of time,
and the expanse of imagination.

My heart has been revived
to the beauty of life,
all because I opened my heart to a *book*.

GRACE

Even as the weight of regret
bends my spine,
my inner light refuses to dim–
holding space for the grace
I've yet to give myself.

With each stumble,
my soul cradles me–
a silent witness to my flaws,
reminding me
that redemption
is a door I can always open.

When forgiveness feels like
a distant universe,
my heart avows,
you are still worthy of the light.

My essence will not abandon me.
Even when I am a stranger to myself.
It holds the mirror steady,
reflecting the truth of
who I can *still* become.

My Steadfast Stars

I cherish the few stars I hold,
constant in their glow.
They do not fade nor flicker,
even as the skies shift
from storms to sunshine,
or when the world falls into deep darkness.

Their brilliance is steadfast–
guiding me when I'm lost;
calming me when the winds howl loudly.

They are more precious than the glitter
of a thousand passing sparks–
bright for a moment,
then gone before they can warm my hands.

In the chaos of fleeting faces,
it is these few stars I trust,
and in their radiance,
I find the way back to myself.

ENOUGH

No amount of shining can change
the shade of the moon to everyone's liking.

Let the brightness fall where it will–
a quiet kiss upon your skin,
meant only for you in this moment–
as you are.

For the moon never pleads to be
more or less.
It does not soften its glow to soothe the eyes
that wish it dimmer– wish it different.
It does not strain its luster for those
that wish it brighter.

It simply drifts in and out of the clouds
with a grace untethered
to the world's demands.

Do not fear the night,
whether you shine or fade within it.
There's a quiet defiance in embracing
the shades of who you were,
and the soft pulse of who you're becoming.

Let the glow settle where it may.
For you, in all your shades of light,
have always been
enough.

CHAPTER SIX

The Attic

Shadow Beginnings

Not all beginnings are born
from the sun and light.

Some creep between the shadows
of grief and brokenness,
waiting to be released from their cage.

THE REAPER IS COMING

Wait and see,
hope whispers.

So I wait,
while my mind spills red constellations–
a thousand warning calls
in crimson shapes.
I think I know the answer.

My heart clings,
fingers desperate, sifting through the air,
searching the unseen for a miracle–
for some spark to keep this pulse alive.

My eyes long for light,
but doubt draws its curtain–
proof and reason shadow my gape.

I challenge the reaper's cold edges,
but haven't you seen the ones who made it?
The ones who escaped your grasp?

He cackles–
a chill that shivers through bone.
Not you, girl. I've marked you.
I am coming.

And I collapse under that certainty,
because I've run out of luck
and am exposed before it.

Hope lies in the corner, silent.
I don't speak to it,
don't feed it with belief.

I don't rub its belly with encouragement.

I lie awake, sleepless,
as the weight of knowing
crushes my chest.

This heart, this fragile heart,
isn't ready to say goodbye.

The Passing

I ready myself for what's to slip away.

The water cascades over me,
washing down the last traces of belief–
scrubbing the corners where hope
still clings, stubborn as fog.

I pound my fists against the glass,
steam curling like unanswered prayers,
and I ask,
Why?

Why pull me close,
only to scatter me again?

I heard the call;
I begged.

What am I supposed to learn
from this undoing?

I gasp between the sobs,
each breath a serrated knife;
tears dissolving into
the draining submission beneath.

I hold my breath,
because even the air stings.

I know what comes next–
the hollowing,
the pain,
the stark vacancy I must face alone.

The harsh, sterile light
will flicker over my sorrow,
and I will pace the path of surrender–
back and forth.

I step from the water's warmth,
naked,
cold,
barren;
detached from what was mine,
standing here again
in a space all too familiar.

My heart protests,
it's not ready
to release what it loves.

I'm not ready to be empty of you.

THE WOMB'S TOMBSTONES

I find myself at the cemetery again,
hands raw from digging in soil
that doesn't want to give.

The stone waits at my feet,
its name not yet etched,
but I know it belongs to me.

The graveyard is quiet,
filled with lives never lived,
rows of untouched cribs,
where their souls sway in the air.

I want to delay it,
want to hold this stone in my hands
a little longer;
pretending it's lighter than it feels;
I can keep it from the earth
if I just hold on tighter.

But the soil calls.
The wind sighs,
it's time.

I kneel,
my knees bruised and bloody
on the soft ground,
and I place the stone

where it must go—
another marker in this garden of grief.
Another silent scream
buried in the ground's womb.

The trees stand as witnesses,
silent and still,
paying their respects.

The sky is dark,
and even when the sun rises—
its warmth is too distant,
too indifferent,
to reach the hollow I've become.

I trace my fingers over the cold stone,
the life that never found breath,
now lying beneath it.

Finality entombs me,
like the last heartbeat
pulsing into nothingness.

I try to stand,
but the silence still holds me—
the weight of it folding into my skin.

I rest my empty hands
upon the piece of earth
that no longer belongs to me,
and I say *goodbye.*

THE CROW'S FUNERAL

The crows all gathered around her;
girdling the broken body.

One poked at her belly,
but there was nothing left,
only hapless dreaming.

She was not dead,
but they mourned her nonetheless.

The crows released a warning call.
The half-dead girl couldn't tell–
was the call to come, or stay away?

But no one came,
and the gathering crows
started leaving one by one;
bidding their goodbyes and
paying tribute in pitied words:

I'm so sorry.

It wasn't meant to be.

Maybe next time.

They avoided where the girl lay,
quickly passing her sobbing stains
and aching stench.

The crows did not speak to her.
The sky and ground were so silent,
and the girl was so
alone
in this death.

WHAT IF

This grief lingers like a heavy anchor,
tethering me to the

what if.

Down in the Muck

In the muck,
sludge sinks deeper into
the swamp of myself,
dragging me
down,
down,
down.

Like a broken mangrove root,
my limbs tangle
in the thick, unyielding quagmire of grief.

I try to reach up,
searching for the reeds in this marsh.
but your imprint tethers me
to the bog of regret.

How much struggle can my spirit gargle
before I just descend?

How will I know the difference
between revival or drowning
if that peace looks the same?

GRIEVING FAWN

I am a grieving fawn,
lost in the thick of the trees,
eyes wide with yearning,
and my heart on its knees.

Through the tangled vines,
where the forest conceals,
I seek a warm embrace,
to mend what death steals.

SCREAMING GRASS

There is no hope
in the grass
that screams
when it grows and is cut
over and over again.

There is no rainbow
in the clouds that
cover the sun.

There is no happiness
when a rain storm floods
a mother's burrow.

There is no comfort in,
it wasn't meant to be.

There is just sadness.

A Silent Carousel

In the abyss between
happiness and despair,
there is *detachment–*
a silent carousel of numbing,
where flickering lights of love
tease and haunt my dignity.

I became stuck on the endless ride
filled with cracked mirrors,
and fractured perceptions of reality.

My spirit, once lively,
is now drained of its vibrancy.

The hard truth I had to accept was that
I didn't know how to halt the spiraling.

The outside became blurred,
and I stopped seeing the hands waving,
the smiles of strangers,
or the luster of laughter.

I was dazed and disoriented,
confined in a forged haze of apathy.
I sometimes would hear a faint call of:
please exit the ride now.

But round and round I'd go;
my ache encircling and repeating.
I finally mustered the faintest of pleas:
I need help getting off.

I Am Not Okay

When they say,
I am worried about you,
I want it to mean more than the words,
that they *feel*
the quiet tremor of my breaking.

I am unraveling,
and all I need is a hand
to tether mine.

I cry the morning into stillness,
silent tears staining the sky–
dabbing at the salt of my misery.

I'm not okay–
wearing grins like borrowed armor.
I laugh for them. I stand.
I pass through the day–
a brittle shell in the flood.

I bend myself into the shape of a smile–
press myself into spaces unfitting,
but the truth throbs in my gut,
I am not okay.

Did you fear I'd spill my grief into your joy,
ruin the fragile calm of your moment?

No, I sat in hours of held breath,
bubbling beneath the surface.

And when I close my door,
I burst into frantic gasps for air,
almost drowning;
choking on the angst.

Still, I pretend for you,
and I can no longer carry
the weight of that silence–
my pretense.

For if you are worried about me,
you should be.

I am not okay.

Noise Complaint

I erupt,
insuppressible,
while they float in their comfort,
wishing I'd stay small.

I expand,
pressing against their quiet walls.
They knock at my door,
entreating my shrinking.

They wish I'd hush it,
fold it away,
and dissolve into something more discreet.

But I can't silence
what demands to be heard.

I can't smother
what needs to breathe.

HIDING SPOT

Do you want to know
where the best hiding spot is?
I mean the one
where absolutely *no one*
will find you?

It's in the facade of pretending
everything's okay.

Your Happiness is Blinding Me

When you are glued
to the floor of darkness,
it seems like everyone around you
is dancing in the light,

and it's so damn lonely.

Storm's Stasis

Sometimes, I wish
the flooding of my tears,
and the thunder of my heartbreak
could stop time,
so I wouldn't have to feel this pain
for just one moment.

Negative

I didn't ask to be the cloud
on this sunny day.
I'm sorry I can't find the silver lining here.
A shadow lingers over me
and I'm trying to find the light.

They don't know
how hard I fight the rope
pulling me down into the darkness.

I didn't ask for my laughter
to be hallowed out–
to be the winter chill
to all your summer smiles.

I'm trying to unlock the door
but the key keeps changing,
and no one tells me why.

I didn't ask for this,

and I can't keep apologizing
for what breaks my heart.

EXHAUSTED

I keep
praying,
wanting,
wishing,
hoping,
dreaming,
imagining,
envisioning,
manifesting.

All I do is close my eyes,
but I haven't slept peacefully in years,
and I'm exhausted
from living
in a perpetual state of
almost.

Broken Puzzle

I grow tired of being a puzzle piece
forced into the wrong spot.
They continue warping my spirit
with every attempt to make me *fit*,

and they wonder why I became broken.

ENVY

You can see it all over me–
the ugly truth of my pain.
It reeks and drips in puddles of rage–

I want what they have too.

Their Wings

I reach out to touch
the threads of their happiness,
fingers trembling with the hope
that perhaps,
some of their joy might unravel
into my empty hands.

But the delicate threads
slip through my grasp,
turning to wisps of air,
as though the very fabric of their dreams
is woven from a substance
I cannot hold.

Their laughter drifts
like feathers on a breeze,
soaring on invisible wings,
while I stand grounded;
rooted in a soil that bears no fruit.
I watch as their dreams ascend to heights
I cannot reach–

as if they belong to a sky
that refuses my entrance.

I search for those wings,
yearning to take flight alongside them,
but all I find are shadows

of what could have been,
and the resounding winds that carry
their happiness far beyond my clutch.

Envy coils itself in my chest,
twisting with grief, I dare not speak.
How can I,
who hold their hands,
also feel this begrudging in my heart?

I want to smile through the throb,
even as I taste the bitterness
of what flies away from me.

My heart aches for the things they cradle,
as if longing
could fill my barrenness.

MORE

I could say that
my hands are full,
yet they still reach into the empty.

I've built towers from my triumphs,
yet they crumble under the weight
of something *missing*.

I wander through days,
aching to find the piece
that fits into the spaces I can't name.

The guilt settles like dust,
coating everything I should be grateful for,
but still, the longing lingers–
a quiet gnawing
for something
more.

NOBODY KNOWS

I wear the light
so no one glimpses
the unraveling within.
They call it strength,
but the truth is,
I've just mastered
how to fracture softly.

WHY

It's been years,
and still I throw questions
into the void,
knowing they'll never land.
Yet, somehow, I keep waiting
for a reason to surface.

I'm not living,
just tallying time–
filling hours with empty gestures,
choking back sobs in closets;
sitting shame-faced on reality.

There are days
where giving up feels like
the only honest thing left to do.

My chest tightens–
joy a distant reverberation.
Every glance, every smile,
feels like a dagger aimed my way.

I can't celebrate their happiness
while I'm drowning in this heaviness–
pulled under by a sorrow
so dense, it smothers me.

Faith is a language I've forgotten.
Hope– a blade that's carved
too many scars in my ribs.

The words escape me now,
and I've long since stopped
trying to speak to a God
who I only meet
in the heat of my anger.

I've screamed at the sky,
over and over,
why?

Why.
Why.
Why.

And though I know the silence
will never break,
it's the screaming
that keeps me from disappearing
into the nothingness.

If You Knew

You say I should loosen my grip–
be less like the tide pulling back.
But you've never stood where I've stood,
never felt the ground beneath you slip.

I think I'd open to you more
if you could see that my need for control
is a reaction, not a choice.
A response to the spaces
where I was left untethered.

I could ease the pressure
if you spoke the language of understanding;
if you knew how scars still scream
beneath my skin,
despite years of trying to mute them.

I revealed
my branded essence,
and no matter how hard I try
to cover the mark,
his shadow lingers
in the corners of my spirit.

You don't understand,
and I feel it in the weight of your silence.

So yes, I wish you knew
that this tightness you feel in me
is not a flaw but a defense,
a necessary tension
in a world that feels too loose.

Control is my shield,
and I carry it
because the world has rarely
felt safe enough
for me to put it down.

CRICKET

I speak,
but no one listens.

I am but an unseen cricket
chirping on a boisterous summer's night;
my truth is just another sound
under the stars,

and no one is listening.

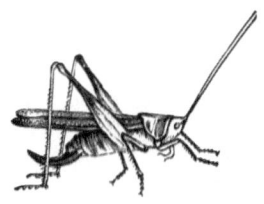

Pity Party

Humiliation cloaked my lips.
I was ashamed to play victim,
to seem self-pitying,
but the truth is, it fucking hurt–
to linger where my name
will never be called.
Rather than just moving on,
I eye the feast from afar,
place my ear to the door,
and listen to the laughter.

Embarrassment breaks my heart,
because I can smell the flavor
of their happiness,
but I will never taste it.

I stand for weeks
outside the circle of conversations,
watching people living from the window.
I desperately yearn
to be part of it all,
to be invited–
to be chosen,

Yet, I remain cemented to the vacant room,
hosting my own pity party,
with no one coming
to drag me out the door.

PERFECTION'S POISON

The weight of expectation smothers me.
I am in a constant state of failure and regret.

I failed to achieve, and I am ashamed.

I don't have it together,
and I am drowning.

My mind is somewhere else–
in between veils–
neither here, nor there.

I am in the void of detachment–
clinging to the numbness of time.

When I rouse,
I am heavy with responsibility,
drained from duty.

I lack creative luster.
I drift within despair.
I scream, but my voice is muffled.

The walls are closing in now,
and the shame is waiting
to suffocate me.

Unbelonging

I often feel like a piece of sky in the ocean;
a comet in daylight;
a lighthouse without a shore.

I often feel like I don't belong.

How can anyone hear my heartbeat
in this city of noise–
remember me in a land of forgetfulness?

I'd like to think that people
might appreciate a stray
amid curated sublimity,
but I seem to remain a wanderer
on this journey of approval.

I think I might be a dreamer lost in reality,
or maybe I'm just the shiver
in a room full of warmth.

So, I just keep drifting, and hiding
like a star shining midday–
unseen and so out of place.

The Sunflower and Thrip

I was radiant,
cheerful,
and kind.

I beamed with the sun,
and smiled towards the sky.

I was gentle.

You latched on,
gritty and unrelenting,
a villain in disguise.

An invisible vandal,
lurking beneath my naivety;
feeding in the shadows of secrecy.

You have left scars–
stained lines of confusion and deception.

My innocence and joy,
plagued by your grime.

I should've known you were a pest,
but I trusted you,
and you spoiled my sweetness.

Lingering

I hate how you still linger
on the vessels of my heart.
I could cut you off,
but in doing so,
I kill the part of me
that loves so deeply.

Silent Burning

I swallowed my roaring ache,
consuming the fury that cracks inside me,
just to keep your world unshaken–
to hide the blaze beneath a surface
that you never cared to douse.

But when the heat scorched through my ribs,
you stood at a distance.
Hands cool, eyes vacant,
as I was devoured by the flames.

I swallowed the sun to keep your secrets,
only to silently scream
as you watched me burn.

Let Go

For too long I've been a withering flame,
holding onto your ash.
It's time for me to let go
and burn brightly.

The Shadow Beneath the Oak

I sometimes feel
as if I am a solitary oak
that has finally stretched its branches,
only to feel guilty
for the shade
it casts upon the ground.

SELLING YOURSELF SHORT

I poured myself into a cup too small–
compressing my worth,
and watched as all the happiness
leaked and spilled
into a sapped puddle,
until there was nothing left to drink.

The Attic

I spent the morning
sifting through the remnants,
dust clung to the corners of
all my wounds.

I stayed, though I'm not sure why–
maybe hoping habit
would hold answers in forgotten places.
I thought if I paused long enough,
maybe something buried deep
would finally rise to meet me.

When I reached
that last untouched shelf,
my thoughts fluttered like startled wings,
searching the shadows for light,
where the things I never dared to face
remained piled.

I sorted through fragments,
too hesitant to clear the air.
No wonder the heaviness lingers.
And after circling the same spaces,
nothing looked any clearer.

Nothing was lighter–
all this holding on
never made the weight any easier to bear.

My Gremlins

Some days, the world feels like a curse—
its smile too sharp.
The sun too bright—
burning holes through my skin.

I retreat beneath the blanket,
where shadows crawl,
and my gremlins stir.

They know me in ways
the daylight never could—
speaking truths
that only the dark dares to reveal.

Their twisted grins comfort me.
Their claws trace the severs of my heart,
and in their company,
I feel more understood
than any good day ever could.

Shattering Silence

It began with a small hand reaching,
only to grasp icy air,
followed by the thudding sound
of a closing door.

You ask how we got here–
it was in the blur of concealed moments,
and salty vapors vanishing into the sky.

I can still feel the chill on my
tear-streaked cheeks,
and hear footsteps crunching away
without a backward glance.

Unanswered questions and inner chaos.
When you have to swallow sadness,
you become a bitter root.

I was told my freckled skin
was kissed by angels;
and they wonder why I have no faith.

I can see the wounds of the world
but, I deserved more than withdrawal.

I vow to shatter that silence–
tear down the walls of shushing.
I can't just turn pages–
I must abandon the book.
There is no saving this inheritance.

Resilience

I have lost.
Lost my breath,
my steps;
my happiness.
I have lost children,
and hope.

But I have loved.
Loved the sky,
the stars;
my dreams.
I have loved my child,
and my soulmate.

I have lived,
and in living there is loss.
There is love.
There is hope and angst.
There is joy and ache.

I am losing.
I am loving.
But through it all,

I must keep living.

CHASING PERFECTION

I could spend lifetimes
warping my reflection–
bending and twisting blemishes,
trying to mold myself into a shape
that is not mine.

In this haze, I go blind;
ignoring the quiet glow within me–
someone else gazes at my edges,
aching to wear them as their own.

I wouldn't wish this curse on anyone,
and yet, I willingly carve myself apart,
piece by piece.

Each second spent longing, criticizing,
is a blade cutting through the heart
of who I am,
yet still, I keep slicing.

If I continue this endless shedding,
what becomes of the light I once carried?
What color will remain
when my soul fades
into a muted shade of myself.

Because the truth is,
no beauty can survive in a world
where we've all traded ourselves away,
chasing an ideal
that only leaves us as dull imitations.

Release

I had to release the venom, drip by drip
from the sadness of my heart.
Burn the fraying roots
of an anger that grew wild,
far beyond its rightful place.

At first, it was easier
to be engulfed in fury
than to mourn.
Just as wearing
a disguise of contentment
was easier than facing the pain.

I couldn't bear the sharp sting of rejection–
couldn't keep unraveling the knots of *why*.
The ache wrapped itself around me, like choking ivy,
its tendrils tightening with each new breath,
forcing me to reckon with the rot
burrowing within me.

I tried to drown it in silence,
bury it beneath the weight of busy hands,
but the ghosts
kept slipping through my fingers,
and I found myself standing among the ruins,
unable to ignore the gaping hollows.

What was once beautiful
had twisted beyond recognition–
I had to let it go.

Pulling up the roots tore me apart,
because sometimes avidity,
untamed and unpruned,
can devour the earth it was meant to nurture.

I had to stop.
I had to watch the fire consume the vines,
and let the ash settle in my grief.

It was only there, amidst the scorched remains,
that I could see the truth–
I needed to mourn the death of something
that had truly belonged to me–
something I loved.

The pain was never the enemy–
it was the clearing–
the necessary cost
to make way for something beautiful,
something that might yet bloom
beyond this pain.

Something I will understand
                                    in time.

Journey to Spring

We are the twirling of departed leaves
separating from their branches.
The warm colors of fall drift to the ground,
and the balmy air shrivels as
a cold breeze slowly wrinkles our grief.

The earth's soft weep for life
turns to silence.

How sentimental death has become—
this transient moment—
a temporary transformation.
It's ugly,
but passing.

The sun begins to rise earlier and set later,
and those cold and dark days will diminish.

Earth's beauty and brightness will emerge,
and the withered leaves of death
are reborn anew.
We will be welcomed
to a new season's luster—
an eternal paradise.

The loss of vibrancy in our spirit,
the agony of losing our hue,
it is the difficult,
but necessary,
journey to our spring.

Dear Debbie Doo,

I'm sorry,
for dimming your smile
until you became a blur;
for crushing your curiosity.

I mistook flaws for fractures
and let the cracks define you.

But I see it now—
the courage it takes
to hold your softness in a world
that gnaws at what's gentle.

You gave without question,
even when the world was a clenched fist.
I should have been there
when your hands trembled—
when the ground beneath you shifted.

Yet you waited, quietly mending,
until I could finally meet you
where you stood all along.

I see you and I thank you
for not giving up—
you saved my life.

Love always,
        Debbie.

A FLICKER

Maybe it was a blessing
you came and went–
like the sweetest kiss on the cheek.
A flicker of magic,
before returning to the embrace
of the stars.

Candle of Hope

The darkness was suppressing.
Like a moonless night,
or a garden where only shadows grow.
I was sad.

But then I saw it–
that candle of hope.
It was barley a flicker–
weighed down by melted wax of insecurity,
but, there was still
a glimmer of flame burning.

I heard a tender whisper of love,
go towards the light.
So I sheltered the tiny glow.

I felt the gentle warmth–
like sunlight on a gray morning.

And as the flame grew,
I too felt an illumination.
It was a shimmering torch
in my chamber of forgotten dreams.

CHAPTER SEVEN

The Garden

And Perhaps

And perhaps,
she would
just follow the fairies
into the forest.

Where dreaming mends
the frayed fibers of her spirit,
and the moss softens
paths long hardened by time.

In a realm where wonders
heal the weary heart,
and laughter blooms
like daisies.

Here, every leaf and
every fluttering wing
is a cradle of comfort,
drawing her closer
to the innocence
she thought
was lost.

THE WEEPING WILLOW

Under a weeping willow,
and atop a patch of gentleness,
the little fairy cries.

She rests her head upon the tree's heart.

As she exhales in wispy strands of sadness,
verdure branches wrap around her–
the weight of comfort offering
protection for her tears.

We may never know why
things so small and pure
become wounded,

but every fairy deserves
a weeping willow's shelter.

LADY MEADOW

In the hushed glimmer of dawn,
the quiet Lady Meadow,
who had been veiled in mist,
reveals her forgotten face
to the newborn light.

When she is kissed by
the marigold sunshine,
dappled buds of daylilies
and buttercups
begin to drape
the gray dormancy.

The critters and flowers whisper,
she has awakened.

The young Lady Meadow cups the light–
washes away the stagnant slumber.

She offers it to her dwellers
with one query,
are you ready to live?

Berry Song

In the thicket's quiet embrace,
fingers paint the earth
crimson and wild,
a reminder that sweetness, too,
springs from tangles–
stretching unseen
through bramble and thorn.

I gather memories like shy rubies,
each one a sun-ripened secret, half-hidden,
and feel the warmth of seasons gathered,
bold and alive against the lines of my hand.

Under leaves thick with the breath of yesterday,
I find the promise of a berry in bloom–
not flawless, yet wholly mine,
its tender skin weathered,
its taste strong and true.
The world sings
through this juice-stained moment,
a pulse of place in every scarlet bead,
and I sip from its wildness,
threading deeper,
each berry a fierce,
tenacious burst of
                    belonging.

HAVE YOU EVER THOUGHT

Have you ever thought
about drifting with the damselflies
under a shelter of stars?
Letting the night's gentle chime
stitch the torn seams of your heart?

Walking among the dew-drenched earth
as it cushions your footsteps
worn by the world?
Letting dreams replenish your tired mind,
as laughter and hope unfurl?

Have you ever thought about going
where every worry breathes unjaded?
Where you allow your eyes to open
to the wonder,
you thought
had faded?

Breeze of Many Wings

When the world woke me up,
clusters of milkweed surrounded me.
Scarlet and golden petals
filled the air with a gentle,
inviting fragrance.

I felt the breeze of many wings–
butterflies, beetles, and bees.
I saw the sun bend the light–
letting me feel its warmth.

This world has energy.
This world is alive,
and I want to live in it too.

BLUE JAY

I was awakened by a blue jay's
song of strength.
She crooned boldly for all to hear,
and did not confine her confidence.

This blue jay had something to say
and would not be silenced.

AUTUMN

I lean into autumn's arms–
letting her warm colors
fold into my soil;
the winds lift what I release.
Rest slips beneath shifting roots.
I am harvest-kissed–
tucked under amber skies.
savoring the ember
before I drift into
winter's slow breath.

Barefoot in the Grass

It's the time of day
where everything is touched by
the sun's golden brush,
and you are *earthing*–
feeling the ground beneath your toes.

Sink into its inviting coolness.
Take a deep breath.
Inhale the life that is around you,
because there is something about the way
the sunlight strikes the trees and the leaves,
or how shadows dance with the wind.

The fresh scent of dew settling
upon the sleepy grass.
The song of a bird.
The buzz of a hungry bee,
The gentleness of a breeze
against your skin.

Dig your feet in deeper to the ground,
imagining roots extending to your soles,
and just let the earth comfort you.

Spring

Earth has awakened from its slumber.

As the thawing of winter reflection settles,
the scent of budding energy surrounds me.
I am filled with vitality and renewal.

There is balance between sun and moon.

I muse to the soothing sounds
of the babbling brooks
and freshly sprouted grass underfoot.
Daffodil sweetness is carried by the breeze.

Spring has arrived,
and I intend to embrace
this season's emergence.

The Cicada Symphony

The cicadas' symphony
serenades the summer day–
a chant of heartbeats
with a sunshine sway.

Flowers bloom in a riot of colors,
and a breeze carries laughter
from distant flutters.

Youthful voices mingle
with the garden's mottled dance;
a fleeting joy,
but certainly not our last chance.

And as the dusky sky settles,
cicadas soften into a sleepy song–
a shimmer of gentle dreams,
rocking the world as night grows long.

Summer Sunshine

Sun-kissed freckles,
painting constellations on my skin,
as I float down a lazy river,
where my daydreams begin.

My heart, a summer pie,
bursting blueberries so sweet,
each bite, a satisfied taste
where play and comfort meet.

You can catch me barefoot,
with a butterfly sway,
as the sun melts away
my worries of yesterday.

Honeybee Hustle

Gather your pollen of dreams.
Let each golden bead mend your heart.
You are the honey of hope,
The hum of your healing.
Buzz your happy beat.
Dance dizzy in the sun.
For your love and joy
will flourish and fuel the world.
And never forget–
you will not be alone,
my sweet honeybee.

In My Dreams

I drift through a world where color spills,
like a sunrise breaking open the sky–
saturating everything with
the pulse of infinite possibility.

Here, judgments are nothing
but fading worries,
swept away on winds of love
that wrap around all things
curious enough to grab it.

Creatures born of imagination
roam untamed.
Like shattered gems–
fairies with wings shimmer,
dragons with scales gleam–
each a flicker of the wildness
that lives in each of us.

We chase our visions with
the freedom of those unafraid;
painting the air with art
that refuses to stay still;
singing melodies that resonate
to the core of the earth.

In this place,
acceptance is like breath–
a reflection that glitters in every glance,
and we dress in the softness of our dreams,
untouched by the weight of shame.

We feast on sensations.
Each taste a burst of joy–
a celebration of the untethered.

Here, life susurrates in colors and sounds–
a serene orchestra
of compassion and creation–
where every heartbeat is extraordinary.

Moon

Moon,
do you see
that without you,
our night sky
would lose its magic?

Your glow comforts us
in our darkest hours,
a reminder
that even in the most distant moments,
we are never truly alone.

You are the quiet reassurance
that light will always return.
You are the commanding tide
that shapes the rhythm of the earth.

You are a silent poet,
writing sonnets across the sky,
read by all who look up.

Though we may sparkle and shine,
it is your resolve that gives us purpose,
turning scattered glimmers
into comforting wonder.

My moon, don't you see,
in your aura,
we find the courage to shine brighter–
to be more than
just distant points of brightness.

Because of you,
our night has a soul.

Love,
Your Stars

SEA OF WILDFLOWERS

What might I find in a sea of wildflowers?

Dandelions of dreams,
or the fragrance of first love?

I might find paintbrushes
soaked in the colors of possibility,
and canvases made of cuckoo petals.

I might find the sun's daughters
and we'd dance under the moon's lullaby.

I might hear the earth's heartbeat,
and snuggle with giant butterflies.

I might have a tea party with the rabbits
or soiree with some snails.

I may attend a caterpillar's ball
and waltz with the bees.

Who knows what I might find
among the wildflower's field.
I'll never know if I don't take the leap.

Raindrop

I'd like to be a raindrop for a day–
fall naturally with ease,
and embrace wherever
fate has me landing.

Spring Air

She is the spring air
that sings plum-scented lullabies,
and cradles the forest with sweetness.

The mother gave birth,
but she is life–

she is the blooming hope
for summer's joy.

Blushing Mornings

Swathed in the soft pinks of sunrise,
I ride atop a lilac dragonfly–
our spirits entwined and
dancing in the sunlight.

We soar above the pillowed clouds,
as bliss whispers freshly
on the breath of this morning.

Dancing Wildflowers

Her spirit is like dancing wildflowers–
untamed and moving
to the rhythm of her own wind.

She sways in every direction;
her smile flowing endlessly.

The world is her meadow
and she does not ask for permission
to bloom.

Magic Mushrooms

In a garden, where the sky wears glitter
like painted moons beneath the trees,
the mushrooms purr and ripen;
they giggle beneath frosted ferns.
I take a bite, spin the world on its side,
turning thoughts into bubbles
that float
up,
up,
up.

They sparkle, these little cap-dancers–
like a mischievous grin tucked into the soil,
each nibble a tickle in the chest,
unlocking doors painted
with forgotten laughter.

The air feels lighter, the heart bounces
like a skipping stone.
I play with the joy of barefoot summers
and hidden nooks.
Where strength isn't taught–
it's experienced.

Here, the child within me stretches awake,
hands sticky with wonder,
and healing feels like catching fireflies
in a jar too small
to contain all this love.

GOLDEN CROWN

She wears joy like a helianthus crown,
with petals in every shade of hope–
turning ordinary moments
g o l d e n.

Openness

Sprawling meadows,
rolling hills, and
starry night skies–

I look for places of openness–
the spaces where I can breathe
and heal away the confines of what
I should be,

and embrace the unhindered honesty
of being
just me.

Can You be a Caterpillar?

Have you ever tried to move more slowly–
like viscous lava,
with its molten patience?

Can you be a caterpillar on parsley–
unhurried and content?

Have you tried to tiptoe rather than stomp?
Drift with the clouds,
rather than race with the wind?

Try flowing with the sweetness
of each moment–
like syrup dripping from a spoon.

Allow your soul to breathe
with slow, quiet
gentleness.

THE FOX

I felt it summoning me,
a fox's siren song.

It weaves through the mossy earth
and wraps me an ivy lure.

The wild,
untamed part of my soul
was set free.

The fox knows the real me;
my elusive, curious spirit
always yearning to scheme
under the stars.

SOMEWHERE NICE

Take me somewhere nice,
where courage blankets
every corner in poppies,
and the scent of olive trees
mingle with the morning sky.

Take me somewhere nice,
where new beginnings
are painted in lavender and celadon,
and the robins sing love poems.

Take me somewhere nice,
where I can rest
in patches of silky groves,
and let the growing earth ease me.

Take me somewhere nice,
where I can be *hopeful.*

Katydid

In the quiet hush of dusk,
where leaves murmur secrets to the night,
she hides, a tender green soul, unseen–
her pain cloaked in the art of concealment.

Yet, if you listen, truly listen,
her heart's rustle stirs within the shadows
waiting to be heard–
shedding her fragile skin beneath
the moon's gape.

She evolves with each cast-off shell–
a shrinking memory–
a wound exposed to the healing light.

The katydid hums.
Change is the soul's quiet language,
and in the unfolding,
I witness beauty emerging– reborn.

In gentleness, in quiet love,
the child within me
finds her way home.

THE FROG WHO SANG TO THE STARS

The Frog sat upon a lily's edge,
croaking a lullaby
only the stars understood.
His song of kindness
flowed with the cool night air.
Each note, a ripple in the sky,
drawing down the gentle glow
of distant clusters–
as if the heavens leaned closer,
and huddled in the comfort of his voice.

His song was not loud,
but tender,
like light rain;
without demand.
It called to the hearts of wanderers,
the lonely–
those with stories– with wounds,
and they came, drawn by the light,
finding their way to the pond.

His voice crooned,
reminding the stars,
and all who listened,
that love grows in the places we tend gently.
When our heart learns *its song*,
the *right* voices
will join in the harmony.

Radiance

In the sun's embrace,
I find the courage
to unleash
my wild heart.

Sunflower Soul

My sunflower soul
leans toward the light,
unfurling with dreams
once tucked away,
now steadily rising–
stretching toward warmth
I once thought unreachable.

In this garden of long-lost joys,
I walk barefoot on soft paths;
the child in me laughing,
reclaiming what was forgotten,
but never truly gone.

The air coos with life,
brushing against scars,
filling them with
a quiet kind of wonder,
as peace gently settles in.

Here, I sow love–
small, resilient seeds
growing in the spaces
I've learned to tend;
turning nettles into strength
and fear into friendship
that holds me firm.

When the sky pours
its golden glow,
I lift my face,
my sunflower soul radiant,
reaching for what
was always mine.

Emerald Land of Hope

In a field of emerald dreams,
wings of butterflies and honey bees
cradle my worries,
as rainbow sunrises
embrace the earth.

Here in this land,
I allow myself to
close my eyes and
hum a song of hope.

That what I wish for–
will be.

Wishes

My body is the vessel of a thousand hopes, strong enough to bear the weight of dreams unbreakable. Each pulse of life carries me further, through mist and light, until I reach the day when the yearning turns to something tangible, real. This path is marked by quiet miracles, a silent promise unfolding in the latent hours– something born from the depths of longing, a presence that fills the empty corners of the heart; my words are winged things now, taking flight toward something brighter. This is the time when all becomes understood, where doubt is swallowed by the rising sun, where I know, deep within my being, that the waiting was never in vain, and what I have wished for takes form beyond wishes. From across the sea of parchment and ink, a voice calls, my pages are paper stars, scattered across the sky of what is now becoming a constellation of faith

guiding me forward.

At the Cottage's Door

The moon rises high,
casting sleepy wisps
through those ageless trees.
My husband, my child, and I
wander down the winding path, well-rested.

Behind us stands
The Enchanted Cottage,
nestled in nature's embrace—
ivy, jasmine, and wildflowers
gently wave goodbye.

The door closes softly,
an oak-kissed threshold,
now a portal we've crossed,
where love thrived
in ordinary, humble moments.

Outside, magic exhales,
the hearth's embers cool,
the garden's singing dwindles,
each room left aglow,
with a haven of tenderness.

Through glowing windows,
the night wraps us in stars;
each twinkle, a farewell
to the wonder we've become.

The air hums with fulfillment,
stories carved in our hearts—
laughter and tears,
engraved into our spirits.

The air sings songs
of healing
and home.

Beneath our feet,
the forest floor softens our steps,
its roots guiding us forward.
The path ahead awaits.

Hand in hand,
we journey on,
with certainty
that magic is real—

it was within us all along.

ACKNOWLEDGMENTS

To my sweet Lily, whose boundless joy, kindness, and wonder light up every corner of my world. You are my magic.

To my love, Dylan, for holding me up when the weight of grief was too much to carry. Your unwavering heart has taught me that even in our deepest pain, love remains our greatest strength. Thank you for walking this journey with me, and for being the best, most patient editor.

To Annalyse, my shooting star— thank you for reading, dreaming, crying, and laughing with me through every step of this book's, and in life's journey. To also have your beautiful artwork in this book, is more than I could've ever dreamed. I'm endlessly grateful to have you in my life.

To The Suriel Tea Club and my shadow friends, I love you for the sisterhood we've created— thank you for holding me through the dark and loving me in the light.

To the Guild and my poet friends— this community has been life-changing, and I'm deeply grateful for your warmth, inspiration, and encouragement.

To my parents, thank you for always encouraging me to chase my dreams and believe in myself.

Thank you to The Enchanted Cottage's incredible cover artist, Felipe. I am also so grateful for your support navigating authorship and publishing.

To the women who have courageously shared their stories of infertility and pregnancy loss– thank you for your strength, resilience, and the wisdom you so generously offer. This book was written for us and to all who are navigating this journey with hope and strength.

Thank you to my incredible therapist, Catherine, and all the healing professionals.

And thank you to those who continue to support me by reading my work and sharing it with others.

I am forever grateful.

About The Author

*Debbie A. Radford is a Houston-based poet whose
writing blends lyrical reflections with nature-inspired
metaphors to explore themes of healing, love, and
resilience. As well as a poet, Debbie is a clinical social
worker and mother, drawing on empathy and
imagination in both her life and her writing.
The Enchanted Cottage is Debbie's second poetry
collection. Her debut collection Desert Dreams was
published in February 2024, inspired by the high
desert of her hometown, Albuquerque, NM. When
she's not writing, Debbie enjoys reading, playing
soccer, and spending time with her family.*

⊙ @debbiearadford   ♪ @debbiearadford

INDEX

www.ingramcontent.com/pod-product-compliance
Lightning Source LLC
Chambersburg PA
CBHW030400130626
46549CB00004B/1575